365
INVENTIONS
THAT CHANGED
THE WORLD

Om KIDZ | Om Books International

Reprinted in 2022

Corporate & Editorial Office
A-12, Sector 64, Noida 201 301
Uttar Pradesh, India
Phone: +91 120 477 4100
Email: editorial@ombooks.com
Website: www.ombooksinternational.com

Sales Office
107, Ansari Road, Darya Ganj
New Delhi 110 002, India
Phone: +91 11 4000 9000
Email: sales@ombooks.com
Website: www.ombooks.com

© Om Books International 2016

ISBN: 978-93-84625-92-4

Printed in China

10 9 8 7 6 5 4

365
INVENTIONS
THAT CHANGED
THE WORLD

Om
KIDZ
An imprint of Om Books International

Contents

2.6 million years ago to 3000 BC

1.	Stone Tools	1
2.	Fire	2
3.	Knife	3
4.	Log Raft	3
5.	Spear	4
6.	Fur	4
7.	Brick	5
8.	Bow and Arrow	5
9.	Cave Painting	6
10.	Flutes	7
11.	Sewing Needle	7
12.	Statue	8
13.	Rope	8
14.	Pigment	9
15.	Preservatives	9
16.	Fishing Net	10
17.	Pottery	10
18.	Language	11
19.	Fermentation	12
20.	Pillow	12
21.	Mortar	13

22.	Refined Salt	13
23.	Axe	14
24.	Irrigation	14
25.	Leather	15
26.	Glue	16
27.	Papyrus	16
28.	Shoes	17
29.	Sundial	17
30.	Wheel	18
31.	Belt	18
32.	Ship	19
33.	Saw	20
34.	Cement	20
35.	Bronze	21
36.	Button	21
37.	Silk	22
38.	Wigs	23
39.	Pens	23
40.	Kohl	24
41.	Tattoos	24
42.	Iron	25
43.	Toothpaste	26
44.	Weighing Scale	27
45.	Ploughshare	27
46.	Dentistry	28
47.	Pants	29
48.	Paved Roads	29

2999 BC to 1 BC

49.	Sewage System	30
50.	Concrete	31
51.	Pliers	32
52.	Dam	32
53.	Soap	33
54.	Toilet	33
55.	Dye	34
56.	Columns	34
57.	Baking	35
58.	Frying	35
59.	Plough	36
60.	Perfume	36
61.	Architectural Arch	37
62.	Ruler	38
63.	Umbrella	38

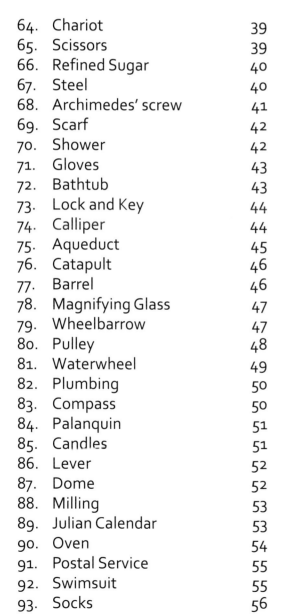

64.	Chariot	39
65.	Scissors	39
66.	Refined Sugar	40
67.	Steel	40
68.	Archimedes' screw	41
69.	Scarf	42
70.	Shower	42
71.	Gloves	43
72.	Bathtub	43
73.	Lock and Key	44
74.	Calliper	44
75.	Aqueduct	45
76.	Catapult	46
77.	Barrel	46
78.	Magnifying Glass	47
79.	Wheelbarrow	47
80.	Pulley	48
81.	Waterwheel	49
82.	Plumbing	50
83.	Compass	50
84.	Palanquin	51
85.	Candles	51
86.	Lever	52
87.	Dome	52
88.	Milling	53
89.	Julian Calendar	53
90.	Oven	54
91.	Postal Service	55
92.	Swimsuit	55
93.	Socks	56

1 AD to 1600 AD

94.	Paper	57
95.	Abacus	58
96.	Toothbrush	58
97.	Vault (Architecture)	59
98.	Hydrometer	59
99.	Church	60
100.	Paper Money	61
101.	Cannon	61
102.	Pretzel	62
103.	Gun	63
104.	Gunpowder	63
105.	Velvet	64
106.	Rocket	64
107.	Dress	65
108.	Spinning Wheel	66
109.	Rifle	67
110.	Lace	67
111.	Spectacles	68
112.	Screwdriver	69
113.	Electricity	69
114.	Pencil	70
115.	Watch	70
116.	Printing Press	71
117.	Corset	72
118.	Teapot	72
119.	Microscope	73
120.	Heeled Shoes	74
121.	Stockings	74
122.	Bullet	75
123.	Hats	75
124.	Clothes Iron	76
125.	Gregorian Calendar	76
126.	Thermometer	77

1601 AD to 1800 AD

127.	Railroad	78
128.	Cork	79
129.	Bowtie	79
130.	Submarine	80
131.	Steam Engine	80
132.	Telescope	81
133.	Tie	82

134.	Barometer	82
135.	Blood Transfusion	83
136.	Parachute	84
137.	Refrigerator	85
138.	Water Frame	85
139.	Razor	86
140.	Mayonnaise	86
141.	Accelerometer	87
142.	Carbonated Water	87
143.	Spinning Jenny	88

144.	Sandwich	89
145.	Smallpox Vaccine	90
146.	Steam Boat	90
147.	Iron Bridge	91
148.	Hot Air Balloon	92
149.	Thresher	93
150.	Cotton Gin	93
151.	Vaccination	94
152.	Battery	95

1801 AD to 1850 AD

153.	Protractor	96
154.	Hang Glider	97
155.	Quinine	97
156.	Tin Can	98
157.	Solar Cells	98
158.	Tractor	99
159.	Reaper	100
160.	Stethoscope	100
161.	Camera	101
162.	Bicycle	102
163.	Suspenders	103
164.	Matchstick	103
165.	Macintosh Raincoat	104
166.	Bus	104

167. Braille — 105
168. Sewing Machine — 106
169. Handbag — 107

170. Harvester — 107
171. Morse Code — 108
172. Telegraph — 109
173. Stamps — 109
174. Suspension Bridge — 110
175. Stapler — 111
176. Aluminium — 111
177. Voltmeter — 112
178. Dirigible — 113
179. Safety Pin — 113
180. Fax — 114
181. Elevator — 114
182. General Anaesthesia — 115
183. Antiseptics — 115

1851 AD to 1880 AD

184. Syringe — 116
185. Gyroscope — 117
186. Bunsen Burner — 117

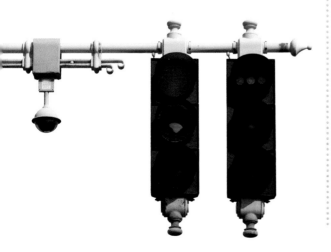

187. Potato Chips — 118
188. Synthetic Dyes — 119
189. Ohmmeter — 119
190. Tuxedo — 120
191. Ceiling Fan — 121
192. Escalator — 121
193. Traffic Signal — 122
194. Barbed Wire — 123
195. Vacuum Cleaner — 123
196. Jeans — 124
197. Hanger — 125
198. Butter Stick — 125

199. Paper Clip — 126
200. Moving Pictures — 127
201. Dynamite — 127
202. Typewriter — 128
203. Cable Car — 128
204. Planned Language — 129
205. Electrometer — 130
206. Mauve — 130
207. Telephone — 131
208. Light Bulb — 131
209. Altimeter — 132
210. Vending Machine — 132
211. Pasteurisation — 133
212. Phonograph — 134
213. Microphone — 134
214. Colour Photography — 135
215. Milking Machine — 135

1881 AD to 1900 AD

216. Metal Detector   136
217. Egg Beater   137
218. Rabies Vaccine   137
219. Skyscraper   138
220. Punching Cards   138
221. Catheter   139
222. Gramophone   139
223. Car   140
224. Light Meter   140

225. Watt Metre   141
226. Electric Chair   142
227. Electric Heater   142
228. Jukebox   143
229. Crescent Wrench   143
230. Radio   144
231. Toaster   144
232. X-ray   145
233. Motion Camera   146
234. Torch/Flashlight   147
235. Cornflakes   147
236. Cotton Candy   148
237. Remote Control   148
238. Aspirin   149
239. Speedometer   149
240. Zeppelin   150
241. Tank   150
242. Dry Cell Battery   151
243. Motorbike   151

1901 AD to 1920 AD

244. ECG   152
245. Popsicle   153
246. Photocopier   153
247. Tar   154
248. Air Conditioning   154
249. Brassiere   155
250. Laparoscopy   155
251. Aeroplane   156
252. Band-Aid   156
253. Bakelite   157
254. Wooden Swimsuits   157
255. Cartoons   158
256. Plastic Surgery   159
257. Teabag   159
258. Zipper   160
259. Hair Dryer   160
260. Chainsaw   161
261. Hot Dog   161

262. Car Phone — 162
263. Architectural Glass — 162
264. T-shirt — 163

1921 AD to 1940 AD

265. Aerosol — 164
266. Sticky Tape — 165
267. Blender — 165
268. Insulin — 166
269. Lipstick — 166
270. Chocolate Chip Cookies — 167
271. Radar — 167
272. EEG — 168
273. The Isolator — 168
274. Missile — 169
275. Hamblin Glasses — 170
276. Computer — 170
277. Yellow Fever Vaccine — 171
278. pH Meter — 171
279. Television — 172
280. Sliced Bread — 172
281. Penicillin — 173

282. Tetanus Vaccine — 174
283. Atom Bomb — 175
284. Snowstorm Masks — 175
285. Richter Scale — 176
286. Chemotherapy — 176
287. Slinky — 177
288. Teflon — 178
289. Helicopter — 179

1941 AD to 1960 AD

290. Velcro — 180
291. Aqualung — 181
292. Magic 8 Ball — 181
293. Napalm — 182
294. Superglue — 182
295. Microwave — 183
296. Transistor — 183

297. CCTV — 184
298. Radio Hat — 185
299. Supersonic Jet — 186
300. Lobotomy — 186
301. Polio Vaccine — 187
302. Kidney Transplant — 187
303. Stairs — 188
304. Pacemaker — 188

305. Ultrasound — 189
306. Microchip — 189
307. Barcodes — 190

308. Hovercraft 190
309. Dialysis 191
310. Communication Satellite 191
311. Autorickshaw 192
312. Video Conference 193
313. Internet 194
314. Laser 195
315. Food Processor 195

1961 AD to 1990 AD

316. BASIC(Programming Language) 196
317. Computer Keyboard 197
318. Heart Transplant 197
319. Glue Stick 198
320. Floppy Disk 198
321. Post-It Notes 199
322. Pet Rock 200
323. Email 200
324. Bedazzler 201
325. Calculator 202
326. LCD 202
327. GPS 203
328. Digital Camera 203
329. Cell Phone 204
330. MRI Scans 205
331. 3D Printer 205
332. Plastic Money 206
333. Space Shuttle 206
334. Genetically Modified Plants 207
335. Flash Storage 207
336. Tamagotchi 208
337. Digital Projector 208
338. Fibre Optics 209

1991 AD to present

339. Text Message 210
340. MP3 Player 211
341. Cloning 211
342. Social Networking 212
343. Blogging 212
344. Dog Goggles 213
345. Edible Food Wrappers 213
346. Instant Messaging 214
347. Flash Drive 214

348. Moss Carpet 215
349. Diet Water 215
350. Metal Detecting Sandals 216
351. Hug Me Pillow 216
352. Portable Chin Support 217
353. Bow-Lingual 217
354. Biodegradable Coffins 218
355. MySpace 219
356. Air Conditioned Shoes 219
357. Android 220
358. Squirt Gun Umbrella 220
359. Snuggie 221
360. Instagram 221
361. Facebook 222
362. Twitter 222
363. Robot 223
364. Mouse 223
365. Ostrich Pillow 224

2.6 million years ago to 3000 BC

① Stone Tools

According to Charles Darwin's theory of natural selection, human beings evolved from an ape-like ancestor around six million years ago. As their intellectual ability and physical appearance started changing, humans also began to create tools by using materials from their surroundings. This ability to create and use tools is what differentiated humans from other animals.

The earliest forms of toolmaking are said to have evolved around 2.6 million years ago. All these tools were made from stone, which is why this entire period is called the Stone Age. The Stone Age is divided into three different eras, depending on the kind of tools that were used in each era. These eras are the Palaeolithic Age or the Old Stone Age, the Mesolithic Age or the Middle Stone Age, and the Neolithic Age or the New Stone Age.

The oldest stone tools are known as the "Oldowan" toolkit. They include hammer stones, stone cores and sharp stone flakes.

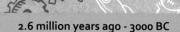

2 Fire

Controlled fire is one of the earliest human discoveries and a crucial one that aided the evolution of humans. Once humans could control fire, they could use it to generate light and heat, to clear forests for farming, to create ceramic objects out of clay and to aid the making of stone tools.

The earliest evidence of controlled fire dates back to the Early Stone Age. Archaeologists unearthed evidence in the form of charred wood and seeds at the Gesher Benot Ya'aqov site in Israel. These are estimated to be about 7,90,000 years old!

Some scientists dispute this by stating that the wood and seeds were not an evidence of controlled fire, but of natural fires that humans took advantage of. However, there may be indirect evidence that supports the discovery of controlled fire 7,00,000 years ago. Around that time, the human brain started growing larger and developing in a way that would be impossible without cooked food. Therefore, scientists conclude that humans must have discovered a way to control fire by then.

3 Knife

Knives were first made by banging rocks repeatedly together in such a way that one of the rocks eventually obtained the desired shape. These knives were very crude and rudimentary. As they were made out of stone, these ancient knives were far from the sharp knives that we use today.

During the Middle Ages, as technology improved and the humans began using steel, more impressive blades were made. They were used as swords during the 13th and 14th centuries. Slowly, these swords were refined and made smaller, eventually making their way to our dining tables!

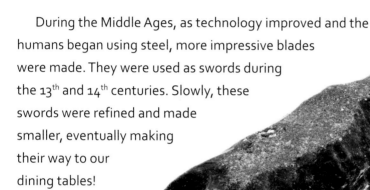

4 Log Raft

The first boat to travel through the sea was discovered around 8,00,000 years ago. Back then, humans had begun to evolve, but they could not communicate. Scientists called them Homo erectus. Homo erectus evolved in Africa and slowly started migrating to other parts of the Earth. These humans travelled to Indonesia, crossing many leagues at sea. This is when they discovered the log raft.

Knowing what plants and tools were available at the time, scientists have tried to guess and reconstruct the watercraft they might have used. Scientists believed that they used giant bamboos that grew in the region.

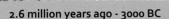

☀ 5 Spear

The development of the spear is considered to be the greatest technological feat in the history of humankind. Engineered almost 5,00,000 years ago in South Africa's Northern Cape province, the spear was developed by the Homo heidelbergensis species of humans. This species used a wooden shaft as the handle of the spear; a hand-chiselled stone as the weapon and mixed adhesives to hold the spear together.

Interestingly, scientists consider the development of the spear as a testimony to the evolving complex reasoning and power of humankind. However, recent studies show that this invention marked an era of peace back then. Before the discovery, early humans acquired territories using violence. When one group invented spears, the other group grew cautious and avoided fighting, which resulted in less tension among communities.

☀ 6 Fur

Have you ever imagined what the primitive humans wore? Did they wear trendy clothes like us? What did they wear when they hunted in the early days? The answer to all these questions is fur. Yes, you read that right!

Fur, which has become a controversial fashion symbol today, was once the only thing that humans wore. Around 70,000 years ago, Neanderthals lived in places with volatile climates. Temperatures changed drastically from very hot to very cold and they had to find a way to protect themselves against the Arctic cold. This led to the discovery of animal skin and its use as clothing. Skins of hairy mammoths, bears, deer and musk oxen were used to make clothes.

7 Brick

Just as civilisation was shaping up, humans felt the need to build houses. We know that most houses are made of bricks. Were these bricks also used by primitive cultures like the Nile, the Tigris and Euphrates, the Indus, and the Huang Ho? Not exactly! Around 8500 BC, during the Bronze Age, humans started making houses of mud bricks.

Mud bricks were made using the clay found on riverbanks. This clay was mixed with straw, kept in wooden moulds and left to dry. After they dried completely, the bricks were left in the sun to bake naturally. Mesopotamian civilisation saw the first kiln-fired bricks. Mesopotamian masonry technology helped build great structures like the temple at Tepe Gawra and the ziggurats at Ur and Borsippa (Birs Nimrud). These buildings were up to 87 feet high.

8 Bow and Arrow

Scientific evidence suggests that the formidable bow and arrow existed around 64,000 years ago in Sibudu Cave, South Africa. However, it is believed that this intelligent invention is much older. The bow and arrow served as both a military weapon and a hunting tool.

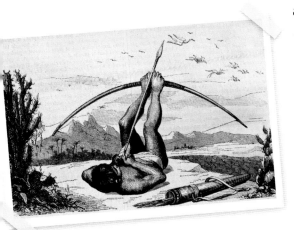

Over the years, different cultures used the bow and arrow for different purposes. For instance, in the Mediterranean region, Europe, China, Japan and Eurasian countries it was used as a military tool. While Europe saw the invention of the crossbow and the English came up with the longbow, the Huns, Seljuq Turks, and Mongols were brilliant, mounted archers. They used recurved bows, which were made of wood and the horns of animals. On the other hand, North American Indians, Eskimos and Africans used the regular bow and the crossbow, primarily for hunting.

☀ Cave Painting

9

Cave paintings can be considered as the primary evidence of the evolution of the human brain. The first cave painting dates back to around 40,000 years in the last phase of the Stone Age. It is also called the Upper Palaeolithic era. Researchers believe that cave art originated in the Aurignacian period in Germany and reached its apex in the late Magdalenian period in France.

Also known as rock paintings, cave paintings were believed to be made by the elders or shamans of the tribe. Early cave paintings were representations of wild animals like deer, bison, horses and aurochs. Abstract patterns and tracings of human hands were also common. It is believed that shamans would retire to the insides of caves to think and draw images of anything that occurred to them.

As opposed to the vast colour palettes and options available for sketching, drawing and painting today, only three colours were available during prehistoric times – red, black and yellow. Even the drawing tools were small and sharpened stones used to scrape on the surface of caves. Iron oxide was used as red paint, manganese oxide as black, and clay and yellow ochre were used as yellow paint.

6

 # 10 Flutes

Most people love musical instruments. Some like pianos; some like guitars and others like drums. Did you ever wonder how old these instruments are? One such instrument – the flute – is around 43,000 years old!

The oldest existing flute was discovered in 2008 in the Hohle Fels cave near Ulm, Germany. It was made from the bone of a Griffon Vulture. It measured around 8.5 inches in length. Evidence of ancient flutes have been found in ancient Greece, Etruria, India, China and Japan. The flutes that were found later were made from boxwood and had six finger holes. Today, flutes are made from metal as well. Also called the Western Concert, these are generally made of brass and covered in silver.

 # 11 Sewing Needle

The first evidence of the sewing needle was found in South Africa. According to researchers, the needle dates back to around 30,000 years.

The first version of the sewing needle was made from bone. Instead of having an eye to sew the thread, this needle had a closed hook. Later versions of the needle were made from wood, ivory and eventually, steel and plastic. Interestingly, the earlier versions were hook-shaped instead of the straight ones that we see today.

12 Statue

You may have seen statues in your neighbourhood, but do you know when the first statue was made?

According to researchers and historians, the oldest statue is 40,000 years old. It was found in the Swabian Alps of Germany and was called "The Lion Man". Another statue, called the "Venus of Hohle Fels", was also found later in the same region. Statues are known to possess great cultural significance. Most statues of ancient Greece, Egypt and Rome are of kings of their kingdoms. One such example is the statue of a striding pharaoh found in Senwosret, Egypt. The Seven Wonders of the ancient world also include the Colossus of Rhodes and the Statue of Zeus at Olympia.

13 Rope

The invention of rope laid the foundation of more complex connecting systems like cables. Can you guess how old the rope is?

The first ever rope is believed to be made 28,000 years ago. Interestingly, Egyptians used water reeds, grass leather and animal hair to make ropes for the construction of the Great Pyramids, which continue to stand strong even today.

Back then, people twisted or braided ropes using simple hand tools like sticks and rocks. "The Spinner" was an ancient method used by rope makers. It involved tying a rock at the end of a stick and swinging it around to weave the rope.

14 Pigment

The use of colour or pigment began with cave paintings around 40,000 BC. While the use of colour in cave paintings was minimal, the proper manufacturing and usage of pigments began in the Egyptian civilisation 15,000 years ago. Natural colours were washed, cleaned, purified and crushed to enhance their longevity and pigmentation. Egyptian Blue was one of the most famous colours during that time. It was later replaced by smalt and then cobalt.

The Chinese developed vermillion almost at the same time as the Egyptians developed Egyptian Blue. 2,000 years later, the Romans started using vermillion. The major contribution of the Greeks to the palette was the manufacturing of white lead, which was used as white paint. It is said to be one of the finest pigments ever made.

15 Preservatives

Most food perishes quickly and loses its taste. To avoid this, preservatives are used. The earliest method of preservation was holding meat above smoke that came from a fire. The smoke would help to dry out the meat and ward off bacteria. Drying fruits and vegetables under the sun was also commonly practised.

Ancient Egyptians used spices and vinegar. They discovered the art of preservation in a strange way. When they buried their dead in the hot desert sand, they noticed that sand would dehydrate the bodies and preserve the flesh. They began using this method with food and called it "drying".

The use of sugar and salt in large quantities also keeps unwanted microorganisms at bay. Jams are an example of this, as are salted meat and fish.

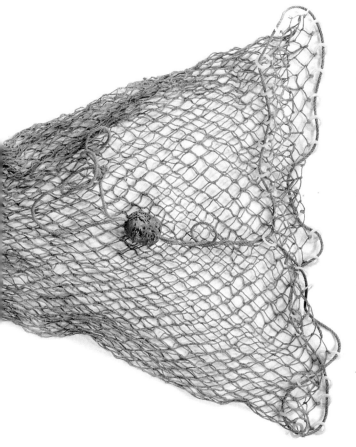

16 Fishing Net

What did the early humans do when they felt like eating fish? Did they jump into a pond and grab it or did they throw a spear in the water to stab it? They did both! Eventually, they figured that they could catch many fish together using a fishing net. So, they made a net using spruce root fibres, wild grass, stones and weights. The oldest fishing net, made of willows, dates back to 8300 BC and is called the net of Antrea.

Rock carvings of Alta, which date back to 4200 BC, hint at the usage of fishing nets during the Bronze Age. In 3000 BC, fishing nets were mentioned in ancient Greek literature.

17 Pottery

The first kind of vessels used by humans was probably some kind of basket made from reeds. These vessels had one major flaw; they could not be used to hold water. To fix this flaw, ancient humans lined their baskets with clay soil.

Once water was drawn with the baskets, they were left aside. The leftover water would get soaked into the clay and dry up, causing it to harden and shrink, giving it the shape of the basket. Furthermore, if these vessels were dried in the hot sand or sun, they would harden even further. This is how the first clay pots were born.

18 Language

We would not usually think of language as something that was formally invented. The truth is that nobody knows exactly how humans began speaking in different languages and it is nearly impossible to find out.

Language can be in two forms – oral and written. Written language is a little easier to trace back. Tally marks are said to be the first form of writing. They were used to keep a count of stock, materials and even the passage of time.

The cuneiform script, one of the earliest forms of writing, was developed in Sumer, which lies in modern-day Iraq. It was written by pressing reeds or styluses into clay tablets to make characters. It originated in the third millennium BC, but by the second century AD, it had become obsolete. During the 18th century, interest in the language was renewed and old texts were deciphered.

Although most languages evolved naturally, a few attempts were made to invent languages. The most successfully invented language is Esperanto, which originated in 1887. It was created by a Polish man named L. L. Zamenhof to unite the world with a common language. Today, more than 1,00,000 people speak Esperanto and over 30,000 books have been published in the language.

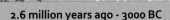

19 Fermentation

Fermentation is a process which involves breaking down substances to create something new. For instance, yogurt, wine, beer and almost every alcoholic beverage is made by fermenting raw materials like milk, potatoes, grapes, etc. Fermenting materials to make alcoholic beverages started in 7000 BC in the Neolithic Chinese village of Jiahu. The earliest form of alcohol was made by fermenting fruit, rice, honey and dates. In 6000 BC, winemaking gained popularity in Georgia, Causcasus.

The first person to associate yeast with the process of fermentation was French chemist Louis Pasteur. He was a zymologist who defined fermentation as "respiration without air".

20 Pillow

The Mesopotamians were the first to start using pillows around 7000 BC. While we like our pillows to be soft and fluffy, Mesopotamians preferred their pillows to be hard and tough. In fact, early pillows were carved out of stones. Researchers believe that people from the Neolithic Age did not use pillows to sleep comfortably but to keep insects from crawling into their mouths, ears or nose!

Inspired by the Mesopotamians, the Chinese, too, began using wooden pillows to keep their heads off the ground. However, unlike Mesopotamian pillows, the Chinese had

elaborately decorated wooden pillows. A softer version of these pillows, which was stuffed with straw, reeds or feathers, was used by the ancient Greeks and Romans.

21 Mortar

Mortar is a thick paste used to stick construction material together. It is used to hold stones, bricks and other construction blocks together. Plaster of Paris is also a type of mortar and was the first to be discovered. It was called the Gypsum mortar by the Egyptians and was used in the construction of the Egyptian pyramids.

Researchers have found evidence of mortar dating back to 6500 BC. This evidence was found in the Mehgarh region of Baluchistan, Pakistan, and the mortar was a mixture of mud and clay instead of stone, mainly because of the abundance of clay during that time.

22 Refined Salt

We already know that salt makes our meal tasty. But it does a lot more! Some countries have fought over it and some have even used salt as their currency. Salt has been manufactured and used since 6050 BC during the Neolithic era in Romania. Researchers have found evidence of salty spring water, which was boiled to extract the salt. It is also believed that salt was directly responsible for the immense and immediate growth of that area.

Salt was used to barter goods in Neolithic times. In fact, slabs of rock salt were used as coins in Abyssinia and Africa. Many years later, Venice fought with Genoa over salt.

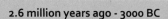

23 Axe

The axe is one of the oldest tools used by humans. However, it looked very different from the axes that we see today. The first axe looked like a sharpened stone. It did not have a handle and was therefore called a hand axe. Axes with handles appeared only around 6000 BC. They were attached to a piece of wood and a length of animal hide was wound around them to hold the axe together.

With the dawn of the Bronze Age, humans began to create axes using metals like bronze and copper. Soon, they began making moulds. This helped to replicate and produce axes on a large scale.

Today, we use axes for a variety of purposes, including carpentry, metallurgy and farming.

24 Irrigation

The concept of irrigation is said to have originated from the river valley civilisations, especially those of Egypt and Mesopotamia. The people would channel the water that overflowed from the Nile and Tigris rivers to their fields. The Egyptians devised a method to measure the level of water, called nilometers. This would help them predict when the river would flood.

Nilometers allowed the Egyptians to prepare for floods. They would divert flood water to lakes via canals and dams. One such canal measured around 20 km!

25 Leather

Leather is considered to be one of the most important discoveries by humans. Egyptian tombs dating back to almost 3,300 years indicate that sandals, clothes, gloves, buckets, shrouds, bottles and military equipment were made of leather.

Early humans used animal hides to protect themselves from forces of nature such as heat, wind, rain and cold. But this became problematic, as the hides would rot in the heat and stiffen in the cold weather.

The initial process of leather tanning probably started out as a mistake. Early humans probably discovered that drying skins out in the sun made them durable and flexible. Rubbing salt into skins, exposing them to smoke and rubbing animal fat on them were some common methods used to create leather. The art of tanning leather was once a closely guarded secret in primitive times, passing only from father to son!

The ancient Greeks contributed a lot towards developing a tanning formula for leather. They began using water and tree barks to preserve leather.

The British started manufacturing leather on a full-fledged basis when they were introduced to it by the Romans. Eventually, the tanning of leather gained popularity and tanneries were set up all over Britain. Some of these medieval tanneries can be seen even today at Tanner Street, Baker Street and Leather Lane in London.

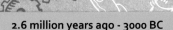

26 Glue

While the glue that we use today is made from chemicals, back in 4000 BC, it was made from tree sap. Archaeologists have unearthed evidence which suggests that ancient Greeks used adhesives for carpentry. In fact, the Greeks made adhesives from egg whites, blood, bones, milk, cheese, vegetable oils and different types of grains. On the other hand, Romans used tar and beeswax to make glue.

A path-breaking discovery in the adhesive world was that of "Superglue". An American inventor, Dr Harry Coover, rejected a substance called cyanoacrylate because he found it too sticky and useless for his research in 1942. A decade later, in 1958, Dr Coover realised that cyanoacrylate was not useless at all! It was then packaged and marketed as Superglue.

27 Papyrus

The discovery of papyrus and its use as a writing material was perhaps one of the most important inventions in the history of mankind. The Egyptians were the first to feel the need of a lighter writing medium after developing the written language. After inscribing on stones for a long time, the Egyptians started using the sap of the papyrus tree to make writing sheets as early as 2500 BC.

Papyrus sheets remained in use till the 11th century AD. The sheets were rolled or made into scrolls for long documents. Scrolls were made of 20 or more sheets whose ends were stuck together. Loose sheets were hardly ever sold. Eventually, books were made from papyrus and called codex. Papyrus, too, had different qualities. Thicker papyrus was used for packaging, while the best quality and finer sheets were used to write religious or literary scriptures.

28 Shoes

The oldest footwear unearthed by archaeologists is a pair of sandals from around 10,000 years ago. The oldest shoes are a leather pair that date back to 3500 BC. However, humans have been wearing shoes for much longer, almost for 40,000 years! As these shoes were made from perishable materials, no evidence remains.

Our bones grow and change according to our needs. Early humans had thick toe bones that would help them walk and climb through rough terrain. Around 40,000 years ago, these toe bones grew small and weak. This is because shoes take the stress away from the toes. This observation helps us understand the historical timeline of shoes!

29 Sundial

The first attempt to record time was made by the Egyptians 3500 years ago. This ancient clock was called a sundial. A sundial can tell us the time accurately by using shadows to record the position of the Sun in the sky.

A horizontal sundial is very common and derives its name from the way it is made. The most common horizontal sundial uses a surface that is marked with lines indicating the hour of the day. The Sun casts its shadow on the style – a sharp, straight, thin rod – forming a shadow on the surface of the sundial. Depending on the time of the day, the shadow moves to different hour lines that are indicated on the sundial.

30 Wheel

The wheel seems like a simple contraption, doesn't it? But it is more complex than what meets the eye. In order to move a heavy vehicle on wheels, the wheels would need to be smooth and equal in size. Their centres would have to be perfectly aligned for the axle to pass through them. The axle would have to fit snugly within the centres of the wheels and yet leave enough space for the wheels to move smoothly.

The first wheel was not used for transportation; it was used for pottery. An updated version of a potter's wheel exists even today. It was only around 300 years after the invention of the potter's wheel that the wheel came to be used for transportation.

The first wheels were heavy as they were formed of a solid, round discus. As a solution to this problem, spoked wheels were invented. These wheels revolutionised transportation and remained in use with minor modifications until the 19th century.

The invention of wire-spoked wheels was a

31 Belt

significant achievement, as it made the wheels even more lightweight. The tyre is another achievement that was invented in the late 19th century. It allows the wheel to move more smoothly as compared to its earlier versions.

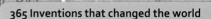

Today, belts are primarily used for two reasons: to keep one's trousers or skirt snug around the waist and as a fashion statement. But the first belt was worn for practical purposes, such as holding tools.

For a long time, belts were commonly worn by men. They started being considered as a fashion accessory for women only in the 17th century.

The modern belt has many shapes and sizes – thin, broad, braided, studded or jewelled. Even superheroes cannot get enough of the belt – Batman's utility belt is one of the most iconic components of his costume!

32 Ship

The first ship was invented around 3000 BC. It was built by tying planks of wood together and stuffing the gaps with dry grass, reeds, and animal hide to make the ship waterproof.

The Egyptians were the first shipbuilders. They made use of sails while travelling downwind and oars while travelling upwind. The Phoenicians built some of the very first warships. Since it was important for the ships to move quickly, they needed several oarsmen to row at once. To serve this purpose, they created a ship called "the bireme" in which the oarsmen sat on two levels, one on top of the other. The Chinese, on the other hand, innovated strong hulls and multiple sails.

The modern ship may not be powered by oarsmen or made from wood, but it still uses elements of all its older counterparts from thousands of years ago.

33 Saw

A saw is a knife-like instrument used to cut through hard materials like wood. It has "teeth" on its edges that help it cut better. Greek mythology states that an inventor called Talos created the saw after observing the jaws of a fish. However, modern archaeology suggests that it was early humans who first came up with the saw.

The very first saws were simply sharp objects with jagged edges. This could be anything from a piece of obsidian to a broken seashell and even a shark's tooth! The ancient Egyptians made the first metal saws from copper. Until the mid-1800s, saws were made by hand. Today, they are made in factories.

34 Cement

Cement is a binding substance that is used in construction. The earliest substance used for this purpose was clay. In Egypt, gypsum was used for the same purpose. The Greeks and Romans used lime that comes from limestone.

There was one big flaw in this cement, however – it needed to be in a dry environment in order to set properly. This was a huge hurdle in the way of underwater or waterside constructions. It was the Romans who discovered the first recipe for hydraulic cement. They achieved it by mixing volcanic ash or crushed brick into the cement mix.

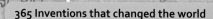

35 Bronze

Bronze was such an important discovery for humankind that an entire era of history is called the Bronze Age. It is the first alloy to be invented by man. Originally, bronze was made by melting copper and arsenic together. By the third millennium BC, tin replaced arsenic in the formula and a new form of bronze was invented.

A big obstacle with bronze was that copper and tin could rarely be found underground together. Thus, the use of bronze involved a lot of trade. In comparison, iron was easily available and therefore more common. That is why the Bronze Age eventually faded away and paved the path for the Iron Age.

36 Button

The first button was made from a curved shell thousands of years ago in the Indus Valley. Buttonholes were not invented until the 13th century AD. The original buttons were simply fitted into loops.

The button was not made to hold together two pieces of fabric. It was used as a fashion symbol and a sign of wealth. In fact, it was said that people could pay their debts simply by plucking an expensive button off their clothes! Later, as more fitting styles came into fashion, buttons helped men and women achieve the right look by fastening their clothing tightly.

37 Silk

Silk is a natural fibre made by dissolving silkworm cocoons in boiling water. A cloth made from silk has a shimmering effect. This is because of the triangular structure of the molecules in silk, which reflect light from several different angles.

Legend has it that silk was accidentally discovered by a Chinese queen. One afternoon, she sat under a mulberry tree sipping some tea. Suddenly, a silkworm cocoon fell into her cup. When the queen tried to pull it out, it unravelled into thin, shiny threads in her hands.

The Chinese were quick to realise that their discovery was significant. The method of creating silk was a highly guarded secret – the penalty for revealing it was death. Traders from far and wide traded silk with other countries for all kinds of riches. In fact, silk was so in-demand that its constant trading led to the popularisation of the Silk Route from the East to the West.

Unfortunately, even the best-kept secrets cannot be kept a secret for long. Some Chinese immigrants carried the secret to Korea. It reached the other parts of the world through various means. Some say that it reached India when a Chinese princess married an Indian prince and carried cocoons in her headgear. Despite that, the Chinese were able to protect the secret of silk for 2,500 years!

38 Wigs

The Egyptians were the first to wear wigs. Most people in ancient Egypt preferred to shave their heads as the climate was extremely hot. However, bald heads were not considered to be attractive. Wigs served a dual purpose of making the heads look like they had hair while also protecting the scalp from the heat.

There were distinct differences between the wigs for upper classes and those for lower classes. The richer sections of society had elaborate wigs that were adorned with silver and gold. These wigs were made of human or animal hair, palm leaves and even from wool!

39 Pens

The first pens were thin twigs which men used to scratch on clay tablets. Pens that could hold liquid ink were made from hollow reeds or straws. Around 500 BC, the first quills were created. These were made by sharpening the ends of bird feathers to make writing nibs.

Quills were widely used for a long time until the first metal nibs were created in the 19th century. The first fountain pen was created in the late 1800s. The main advantage of this pen was that it could hold a large amount of ink, thus eliminating the need to constantly refill it.

Today, apart from fountain pens, there are several, widely used varieties such as ballpoint pens, roller ball pens, felt pens and pens with ceramic nibs.

40 Kohl

Kohl is a form of eye makeup. It is not just used as a cosmetic; it is a coolant and is also believed to protect children from evil eyes. Kohl was historically worn in Egypt, South Asia, the Middle East and other parts of Africa.

The Egyptian recipe for kohl consisted of stibnite, which is a sulphide of antimony. One way to make kohl was the dip-dry method, in which a small square of muslin was repeatedly dipped into sandalwood paste and left to dry in the sun, forming a wick. This wick was used to light an oil lamp. The soot thus formed was used as kohl.

Kohl gained popularity in the west only in the 1950s, when women began to apply makeup more liberally than before.

41 Tattoos

Tattooing is the art of inserting dye below the surface of the skin permanently. The oldest evidence of tattooing comes from Otzi the Iceman, who lived around 3300 BC. He had a total of 57 tattoos across his body. The placement of these tattoos suggest that they were not decorative, but therapeutic – perhaps to heal arthritis.

Many different methods of tattooing have been used through the ages. A common method was to cut open the skin and rub it with ashes. Rubbing salt into open wounds would also ensure that the scars didn't fade, thus forming a different kind of tattoo. Today, indelible ink is inserted into the dermis of the skin through special needles to create tattoos.

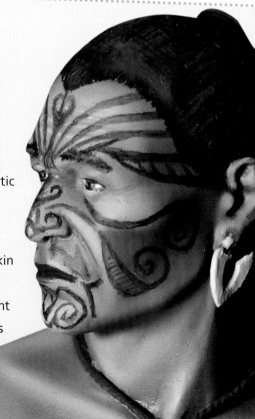

42 Iron

As iron is available in abundance, it is not exactly an invention. However, this versatile metal has been widely used throughout the ages and its use for various purposes could be called a discovery in itself.

The Iron Age was an important era in history when humans made great progress in building tools and implements. Today, it's safe to say that the world would undergo greater suffering if we ran out of iron, instead of gold or silver.

Iron was probably first discovered when early humans tried to burn the ore and found that it melted at a high temperature. Soon, they began replacing bronze with iron in instruments and implements.

It is widely believed that the Asians first came up with the concept of iron smelting, slowly spreading their methods across the world. A common place for smelting iron was a bloomery. Here, the iron was heated until it became a spongy mass. This mass was then hammered into the desired shape.

Over the years, improvements in furnaces and processes led to the discovery of different types of iron, like cast iron, pig iron, etc.

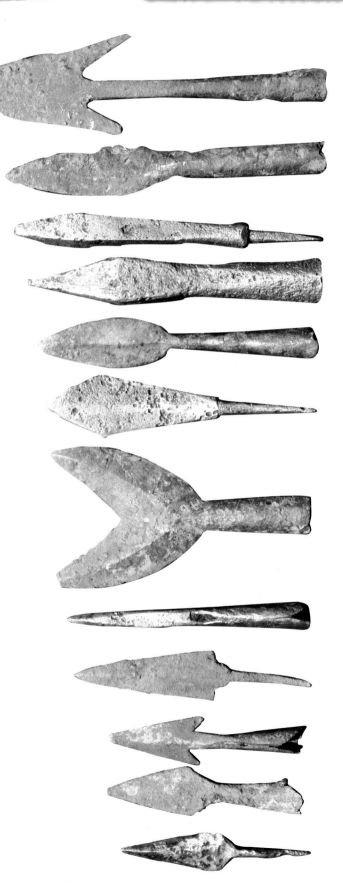

43 Toothpaste

It is believed that the Egyptians began using a paste to clean their teeth around 5000 BC. Ancient Greeks and Romans are known to have used toothpastes, and people in China and India first used it around 500 BC. Ancient toothpastes were used for keeping teeth and gums clean, whitening teeth, and freshening breath. The ingredients of ancient toothpastes differ from the ones that we use today. Back then, ingredients like ash and burnt eggshells were combined with pumice to make toothpaste! The Greeks and Romans favoured more abrasiveness, and used crushed bones and oyster shells. The Romans added more flavouring for good breath as well as powdered charcoal and bark. The Chinese used a wide variety of substances such as ginseng, herbal mints and salt.

Modern varieties of toothpaste gained popularity in the 1800s. The early versions contained soap. Chalk was included in the 1850s. Betel nut was included during the 1800s. In 1873, Colgate mass produced the first toothpaste in a jar. In 1892, Dr Washington Sheffield created the first toothpaste in a collapsible tube. Currently, the use of fluoride has increased in toothpastes as it has been found to reduce cavities.

44 Weighing Scale

Weighing scales are said to have originated during prehistoric times. It is believed that the first weighing scales were used in the Mesopotamian Civilisation in 4000 BC. For the purpose of bartering, a weighing scale was needed. The first weighing scale of the modern era was built and designed by Leonardo Da Vinci during the late 15th century. In 1897, the first scale with indicators was built. The indicating scales appeared in 1940.

Soon after, the electronic weighing scale was designed and perfected, which continues to rule the market till today.

45 Ploughshare

A ploughshare is a part of the plough. It is the cutting or leading edge of a mouldboard that closely follows the "coulter" or the ground-breaking spikes when ploughing.

Triangular-shaped stone ploughshares were discovered at the sites of Majiabang culture around Lake Taihu. These ploughshares date back to 3500 BC. Ploughshares have also been discovered at the nearby Liangzhu and Maqiao sites that date back to around the same period.

The ploughshare is often a hardened blade dressed into an integral mouldboard. This is done by a blacksmith.

46 Dentistry

The first known case of treating tooth related problems dates back to 7000 BC, where the Indus Valley Civilisation shows evidence of treating tooth decays. The first method used for treating tooth decay involved bow drills. These tools were used for wood works as well as treating tooth problems!

The Sumerians thought that worms made small holes in teeth and hid inside them. The idea of a worm residing in teeth and causing dental pain actually lasted until the 1700s!

In ancient Greece, Hippocrates and Aristotle wrote about treating decayed teeth and extracting them to keep the pain away. During this time, extraction was done using forceps, which were used to treat several diseases during the Middle Ages.

During the 18th century, dentistry took a scientific turn. It was revolutionised during the late 18th and 19th centuries. For many centuries, rich patients would get gold fillings in their teeth as a symbol of wealth. False teeth made from porcelain were invented in 1770. Amalgam was first used in Europe around 1820.

The dentist's chair was invented in 1790 by Josiah Flagg.

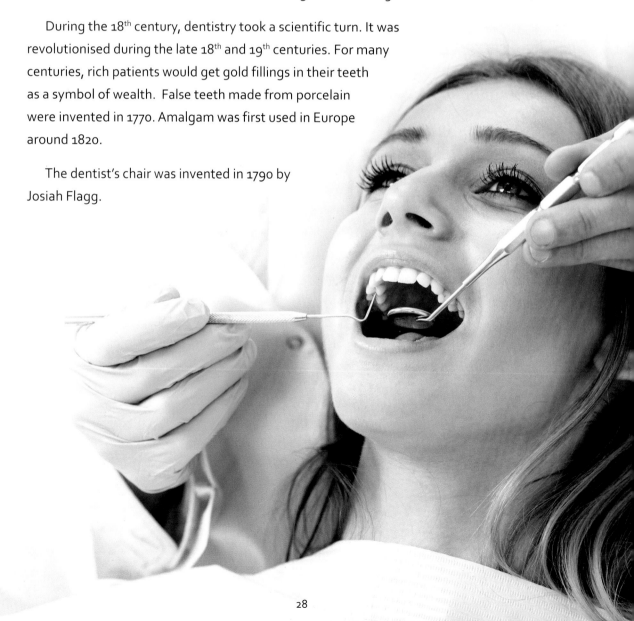

47 Pants

Archaeologists Ulrike Beck and Mayke Wagner excavated two ancient graves in a cemetery in Xinjiang, China. Among the remains, they discovered two pairs of well-preserved, woollen pants. Research shows that these pants were between 3,000 and 3,300 years old, making them the oldest-known pair of trousers to be discovered.

This time period corresponds with the rise of "mobile pastoralism" in Central Asia, where nomads began moving their herds across the land on horseback. Tunics and robes were not comfortable or suitable for long, bumpy rides as well as for battles. As a result, pants were created.

48 Paved Roads

Around 2500 BC, a road built in Egypt by Pharaoh Cheops is believed to be the earliest paved road on record. It is 1,000 yards long and 60 feet wide. It led to the site of the Great Pyramid. Since it was used only for this job and never for travel, Cheops's road was not, in a true sense, a road like the later trade routes, royal highways and impressively paved Roman roads.

Those who built roads during the late 1800s depended solely on stone, gravel and sand for construction. Water would be used as a binder to give some unity to the road surface.

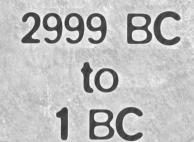

49 Sewage System

Even though it may be awkward to talk about, all of us have to answer nature's call. Today, most civilised people use indoor lavatories. Have you ever wondered what happens after you flush? Where does all the sewage go?

In order for you to have the luxury of a toilet within your own home, a system of pipes and channels need to be in place first. The first sewage systems were not quite systems at all. They were toilet-like cavities that drained to channels just outside.

The first instance of a sophisticated sewage system comes from the Indus Valley civilisation which flourished around 3000 BC. Each house had a bathroom and latrine. These were connected to sewers that led to the river.

One of the greatest wonders of ancient architecture is the Great Bath in Mohenjo Daro. It was a public bath, not unlike the swimming pools of today. It had a hole at one end which was used to drain the water out.

50 Concrete

The word concrete is derived from the Latin word "concretus", which means condensed or compact. Concrete is a mixture of water, cement and certain other materials. It is normally strengthened by using rods or steel mesh before it is poured into moulds to form blocks. Interestingly, the history of concrete dates back to Rome around 2,000 years ago. Concrete was essentially used in the construction of aqueducts and roadways in Rome.

Romans are known to have used concrete for building roads on a large scale. Interestingly, they built approximately 8,500 km of roads using concrete. Concrete is a very strong building material. Historical evidence shows that Romans used several materials such as quicklime, pozzolana and an aggregate of pumice, substances like animal fat, milk and blood, as mixtures for building concrete.

John Smeaton, an engineer, made concrete by mixing coarse aggregate of pebbles and powdered brick, and added this mixture to cement. This is the mixture that we continue to use even today. In 1756-59, he built the third Eddystone Lighthouse in Cornwall, England. It was during the planning of this lighthouse that Smeaton invented the hydraulic cement. Another major development occurred in 1824. An English inventor, Joseph Aspdin, invented Portland cement by burning grounded chalk and finely crushed clay in a limekiln until the carbon dioxide evaporated, resulting in strong cement. The first systematic testing of concrete took place in Germany in 1836.

51 Pliers

No one knows for certain when pliers
were invented. They were probably invented
out of necessity – humans felt the need of tongs to
help them work with hot fires. With the dawn of the Metal Age, hot
fires turned into blazing hot furnaces. Makeshift wooden pliers would no
longer do. Thus, the first bronze pliers were made in circa 3000 BC.

Today, we have pliers of varying sizes that are used for various purposes. There are surgical pliers, dental pliers, laboratory pliers, kitchen pliers and even jewellery pliers!

52 Dam

Like many other ancient inventions, the Egyptians built the first dam. This was a simple dam made of rock and gravel which resisted the force of water simply with its weight. However, this dam was not very effective as water eventually managed to trickle through the rock.

The Mesopotamians had better luck with their dam, which was made of soil and clay. Wooden dams are also believed to have been constructed.

The Romans built the first concrete dam in 100 BC, but it was only in the 17th century that the Spanish perfected the art of making dams. They travelled around the world, taking their building methods with them and sharing their knowledge with the rest of the world.

53 Soap

Soap has been used since 2800 BC and was invented by the Babylonians. Back then, it was simply a cake made from animal fat. Do you ever wonder how humans came to the realisation that rubbing themselves with animal fat would make them cleaner? Legend says that animal sacrifices might be the reason. People noticed that fat ran into the river water, forming a clay-like substance that left their clothes cleaner when they washed them with that water.

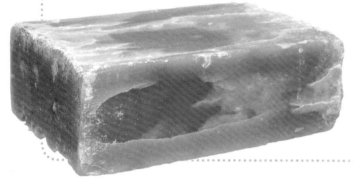

Even though soap is such an ancient invention, liquid soap and shower gels did not come into existence until about a hundred years ago.

54 Toilet

The first toilets were nothing more than holes in the ground. However, toilets with a flushing system are not a recent invention. The first such toilets were found in the ancient Minoan, Egyption and Harappan civilisations.

The first instance of the modern flush toilet that we know today appeared in the 16th century. It was designed by Sir John Harington, who installed one for his godmother, Queen Elizabeth I. However, she refused to use it as she found it too loud!

As the population increased, so did the production of sewage. This was when the toilet gained popularity.

55 Dye

Until the 19th century, all dyes were made from natural substances. Colours in the red, brown and orange families, which are easily found in nature, were the very first dyes to be used by humankind. The process for creating these dyes was simple – the source of the dye, along with the fabric to be dyed, would be boiled in water until the colour transferred from the source to the fabric.

Colours like blue were also developed with the help of flowering plants. Indigo was one of the most widely produced and sought-after natural dyes. However, it wasn't until much later, in 1856, that the first man-made dye was discovered.

56 Columns

A column or pillar is an architectural structure that distributes the weight of a heavy structure onto the ground below it. This allows the use of ceilings without the need of actual solid walls to support it. There are instances of columns found in ancient architecture, including that of the Egyptian, Assyrian and Minoan civilisations. However, it was the Persians who built some of the most ornate and beautiful columns.

During the Middle Ages, the use of columns diminished greatly. They reappeared in Renaissance architecture in the 15th century.

57 Baking

Baking was one of the earliest forms of cooking. Ancient humans would crush grains and mix them with water to form a paste. This paste would be laid on a hot rock, which would cook it into some kind of flat bread. The Romans were known to be very keen bakers. They had lavish parties and their spreads would include new and innovative baked foods.

During the Middle Ages, consuming pastries and baked products became a sign of prestige. The rich ate bread made from refined flour, whereas the poor had to settle for coarse bread. It was only during the Industrial Revolution of the 18th century that baked goods became available just as easily to the common folk.

58 Frying

While frying is an ancient invention, it was only practised by a few civilisations, like the Egyptians and Mesopotamians. This is because other civilisations had not discovered methods by which they could crush the seeds to extract oils. It is believed that fried cakes were eaten in Egypt since 2500 BC!

Isn't it a strange idea that cooking something in oil and fat would make the food tasty? Native Americans thought so, too! When the Europeans settled in the Americas, the natives were repulsed at the idea of frying their food. However, the method found its way into their cuisine. Gradually, people began frying meats and the method soon became popular in cuisines around the world.

59 Plough

The practice of irrigation and the systematic plantation of crops began a long time ago. The first evidence of planned farming dates back to the Mesopotamian era. The plough is a very important tool in farming; its earliest evidence dates back to 2000 BC. Interestingly, early British Law directed ploughmen to use only those ploughs that were constructed by them.

Simple ploughs were developed from handheld hoes created by the Egyptians. These ploughs were pulled by oxen, camels and elephants. However, some of these methods have been frowned upon by historians because they involved cruelty towards animals. Till around the 17th century, farmers would tie the ploughs to the tail and horns of the animals.

60 Perfume

The art of making perfume began in the Mesopotamian era around 2000 BC and was continued with much fervour by the Romans and the Persians. The word perfume has Latin origins and comes from the word "perfumare" which means "through smoke".

According to historians, a Mesopotamian woman called Tapputi distilled flowers, calamus and oil to make perfumes in 2000 BC. The process involved filtering and mixing these ingredients with other aromatics and setting them aside for a long period of time.

The world's oldest perfumes were discovered in 2005 by archaeologists in Cyprus. These perfumes are older than 4,000 years. Evidence suggests that they had been manufactured in a 43,000 square feet perfume factory. These perfumes were made from flower extracts mixed with spices like almond, bergamot and myrtle.

61

Architectural Arch

The earliest evidence of architectural arches used for gates dates back to the Bronze Age. This evidence was unearthed in the city of Ashkelon, (now in modern day Israel), in 1850. True arches or perfectly round arches were often used for underground buildings like the drainage systems in Mexico, the Levant and ancient Near East.

The Romans were the first to start using arches extensively in their structures. They learnt the art of constructing arches from the Etruscans and, after much improvisation, used the arches for above-the-ground structures like bridges, aqueducts and gates. The triumphal arch was invented by the Romans and used as a military monument throughout their civilisation.

62 Ruler

Measurements are crucial to building and construction. Thus, rulers have existed for several years. Initially, they were made of ivory and wood. The earliest exidence of a ruler was found in the remains of the Indus Valley civilisation. It dates back to around 2400 BC.

Before we had this instrument, people used their body parts for measuring things. For example, a cubit was the length of a man's arm from the elbow to the tip of his middle finger. However, this system had its drawbacks – everyone's arms are not equal in size! The person who took the measurements would ideally have to build it himself/herself.

Thus, with the invention of the ruler, a common standard unit of measurement was introduced which would be the same for all.

63 Umbrella

Today, we cannot imagine living without fans and air conditioners to keep us cool. They make our lives more bearable. For the people who lived during the ancient times, the umbrella was such an invention. It greatly improved the quality of their lives simply by providing them additional protection from the elements of nature.

The umbrella was first used as a shade against the sun. This concept later evolved into the parasol. However, one difference between an umbrella and a parasol is that a parasol is usually held over another person instead of holding it over oneself.

The first umbrellas were symbols of rank and royalty. In ancient Egypt, fair skin was associated with high class. That is why the kings and the highest nobility had their servants hold umbrellas over their heads as they walked.

64 Chariot

Archaeologists believe that chariots were invented in 2000 BC in the ancient Near East civilisations. More prominent evidence of full-spoke chariots were found from the remains of buried chariots at the Andronovo sites in the Sintashta-Petrovka Eurasian culture.

Double-axled wagons and chariots were invented in late 2000 BC in Southern Mesopotamia. The lighter, horse drawn chariots played a significant role in Mesopotamian warfare.

The horse drawn, wheeled vehicle probably originated in Mesopotamia around 3000 BC. The earliest depiction of vehicles in the context of warfare can be found on the Standard of Ur in southern Mesopotamia, dating back to 2500 BC.

65 Scissors

Historians suggest that modern scissors were invented in Rome around 100 AD. However, a primitive pair of scissors was made in Egypt in 1500 BC. It was called the spring scissors because the handles of its bronze blades were connected with flexible, curved, bronze spring. When the handles were squeezed together, the spring ensured that the blades stayed aligned. In fact, Europeans used the spring scissors until the 16th century. The bronze spring scissors were widely used in China, Japan and Korea too.

66 Refined Sugar

Refined sugar, as we know it today, refers to the pure white crystals of sugar that we usually mix into our beverages. The sugarcane plant can be crushed to release juice. The people of ancient India discovered that by boiling this juice, it would reduce to form small, rocky particles.

Initially, sugar was so rare that it was called "white gold". But as sugar spread around the whole world, newer and cheaper refining methods were discovered, thus bringing down the cost.

Today, the world consumes a total of about 120 million tonnes of sugar every year. This figure is steadily rising by two million tonnes a year.

67 Steel

The first evidence of steel manufacturing can be traced back to 2000 BC at an archaeological site in Anatolia. During the same era, steel was also being manufactured in East Africa. The alloy was also used to make weapons like the falcata in the Iberian Peninsula. Noric steel was used to make artillery for the Roman military. The Chinese, too, used quench-hardened steel to make weapons in the Warring States period, i.e., from 400 BC to 220 BC. The Han dynasty produced steel by melting wrought iron and cast iron together, which produced the best carbon intermediate steel in the first century.

It has been speculated that steel was produced in iron smelting factories and bloomeries in the ancient era. The Spartans also produced steel extensively in 650 BC.

68 Archimedes' screw

The Archimedes' screw or the screw pump is an ancient tool used to transfer water from low-lying water bodies to farms. Greek mathematician Archimedes of Syracuse invented the screw in 300 BC.

Apart from irrigation, the Archimedes' screw was used to drain out land covered by sea water in the Netherlands. Here, water was pumped out from a shallow part of land covered by sea. This water was then used for irrigation. The Archimedes' screw was used by the Assyrian King Sennacherib from 706 to 608 BC. Even the classical author, Strabo, describes that screw pumps were used to water the Hanging Gardens. Screw pumps evolved when German engineer Konrad Kyeser installed the crank mechanism in them.

 69 Scarf

Rome introduced the world to scarves. Men started using "sudarium" or "sweat cloth" by tying them to their belt or wearing them around their necks in the third century BC to wipe their necks and faces during summer. Eventually, women began using scarves made of wool, pashmina and silk, and made them a fashion statement.

Chinese warriors wore cotton scarves to identify themselves during Chinese emperor Cheng's rule. Following the example, soldiers in Croatia wore scarves which were decorated as per their ranks. The officers in the Croatian army wore silk scarves while the others wore plain cotton scarves.

70 Shower

The Romans believed in bathing several times a week and hence followed the Greeks when it came to making showers. The earliest showers known to humankind were built by the Greeks in 800 BC. The Greeks built large rooms meant for showering which resemble the locker rooms of today. These shower rooms were meant for both the elite and commoners, and were found in the city of Pergamum.

The Romans followed this system and improvised by making lead pipes to both pump in and pump out the water. They also made a complex and intricate sewage system to cater to the sanitation needs of society.

71 Gloves

Gloves are considered to be quite unique. Herodotus, in "The History of Herodotus" (440 BC), mentions how Leotychides was incriminated by a glove or "gauntlet" containing silver that he received as a bribe. There are occasional references to the use of gloves among the Romans as well. Pliny the Younger (c. 100 BC), who worked as his uncle's shorthand writer, wore gloves during winter so that his work wouldn't get affected.

During the 13th century, gloves were worn by ladies as a fashion ornament. They were made of linen and silk. It was in the 16th century that gloves grew more popular when Queen Elizabeth I set the fashion for wearing them.

72 Bathtub

According to historians, Romans are known to be the champions of bathing. It was the Romans who first began to bathe everyday in public baths. Early plumbing systems provided for baths date back to 3300 BC. However, the evidence of actual bathtubs dates back to 500 BC in Rome.

The first personal bathtub was discovered on the Isle of Crete with a 5-feet-long pedestal made with hardened pottery. The Romans also used marble for tubs, and lead and bronze for pipes, which created a complex sewage system.

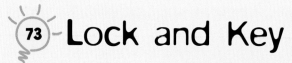

73 Lock and Key

The earliest lock and key device, dating back to around 4,000 years, was found near Nineveh, the capital of ancient Assyria. The ancient Egyptians were known to use wooden pin locks. These locks had a series of pins inside them. When the right key was inserted, it would push the pins aside, allowing the lock to open.

The first metal locks appeared towards the end of the first century. Metal keys, too, were used. The Romans were known to lock their safes and wear their keys on their fingers as rings. This not only kept them safe, but also allowed them to show off the fact that they had valuables that were locked away.

74 Calliper

Calliper is a measuring instrument that resembles a compass. It is very useful for minute measurements. The oldest specimen was found in a Greek shipwreck near Italy. It was made in the sixth century BC. Thus, the Greeks and Romans were the first ones to use callipers.

A bronze calliper from the ninth century AD was found with an inscription that helped to date it. It could measure distances as small as a tenth of an inch.

The modern calliper was invented in 1851 by an American named Joseph R. Brown. It can measure even a thousandth of an inch.

75 Aqueduct

Aqueducts refer to the channels or tunnels that carry water from one place to another for easy usage. The river valley civilisations of India, Persia, Egypt, etc., had plumbing systems in place to bring water into people's homes.

However, the aqueduct system of ancient Rome is said to be one of the most sophisticated examples of ancient plumbing. It consisted of channels that carried water from lakes and rivers to homes, public baths and even to farms. These channels were constructed from terracotta, stone, wood or metal.

Over the course of half a century, 11 aqueducts were built in Rome. Some of these transported water from a distance of around 100 km. The aqueducts were built at a slightly downward slope. Thus, gravity was enough to push the water through them.

Most of the aqueducts were built underground. But a 50 km stretch of one particular aqueduct was built over a valley in the form of a stone arch. Many of Rome's aqueducts fell out of use due to a lack of maintenance. Some were destroyed by enemy attacks.

The aqueducts were responsible for Rome's thriving population and the Romans certainly felt their loss. After the aqueducts fell out of use, the Roman population fell from a million to around 30,000.

76 Catapult

Historically, the catapult was a weapon that used to fling heavy rocks over a great distance. The story of its invention is rather interesting. Dionysius the Elder of Syracuse, Greece, was one of the worst tyrants of the ancient world. He wanted to build a new weapon to strengthen his army. So, he invented the catapult around 400 BC.

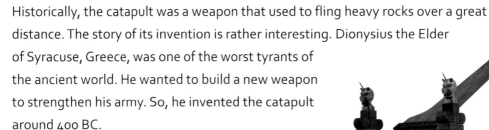

Another kind of catapult, the "ballista", was derived from the original design. It was built to shoot arrows instead of heavy loads. The Romans added wheels to the catapult so they could move it around easily.

77 Barrel

In comparison to the inventions of today, the idea of the barrel being a revolutionary invention seems rather ridiculous. However, before the barrel came into the picture, clay pots were used to transport goods. These were not only fragile, but heavy to carry to and fro.

On the other hand, the barrel had a rounded shape, which meant that it could be rolled. Its straight top and bottom meant that it could be stacked easily. It also had handles and in some cases, even wheels.

The rounded sides of the barrel were built using the same methods used to build boats, as discovered by the ancient Egyptians and Phoenicians.

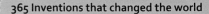

Magnifying Glass

The magnifying glass is said to have been invented in 1250 by an English friar named Roger Bacon. However, references to similar devices have been found in many instances throughout history.

In 423 BC, Greek playwright Aristophanes wrote a play called "The Clouds" in which magnifying glasses were sold for the purpose of starting fires.

Four hundred odd years later, Pliny the Elder described the same effects with a glass globe filled with water. Both he and Seneca the Younger noted that it could be used to read tiny letters.

Wheelbarrow

Surprisingly, during ancient times, wheelbarrows were not widely used for agricultural and farming purposes. However, they seemed to be a common instrument for carrying light to medium loads at Greek construction sites.

The oldest clue of the existence of a wheelbarrow comes from an ancient Greek list of building supplies. It describes an item called the "monokyklos", which means "one-wheeler".

However, there is no way to ensure if they were indeed referring to the wheelbarrow. Thus, several historians believe that it was the Chinese who actually invented the wheelbarrow around 100 BC.

80 Pulley

The pulley is yet another invention that stems from the creation of the wheel. It uses a wheel, axle and a belt or rope to pull heavy loads with little force. The wheel is placed on the axle. It controls the movement and direction of the rope.

The pulley was first mentioned in a Greek text from the fourth century BC. Evidence also states that in 1500 BC, the Mesopotamians used simple rope pulleys to hoist water from wells. However, it is very likely that the pulley existed much earlier, even though there isn't enough evidence to support the theory. The prehistoric monument Stonehenge, is believed to have been built using pulleys.

A pulley that uses one wheel only is called a simple pulley. A compound pulley distributes the weight across several wheels, thus making it possible to haul even heavier weight with considerable ease. Greek inventor Archimedes is said to have invented the compound pulley.

It is said that he had the idea for the compound pulley when he was watching ships being hauled towards the port by several men. With the compound pulley he made, he managed to haul an entire warship with its crew using only the pulleys and his own strength. This remarkable feat led him to say the famous words: "I could even move Earth if I had a place to stand!"

(81) Waterwheel

The wheel is an iconic invention because of its many applications. One such application was the waterwheel. Initially, it served one of two purposes – irrigation and power generation. It was moved manually with the help of animals or by the water's current.

Waterwheels have grooves on them. When water strikes the wheel, the grooves catch it. The weight of the water in the grooves causes the wheel to move, creating kinetic energy. The wheel then deposits the water into channels for irrigation. The movement of the wheel itself can be used to churn or move machines, like those in mills.

Waterwheels were simultaneously invented in different parts of the world. The Greeks and the Romans first created the waterwheel between the third and first centuries BC. By the first century AD, the Chinese were also using horizontal waterwheels to power their mills.

Even though waterwheels are not widely used today, the modern invention of a hydraulic turbine is heavily derived from it. Water sets the turbine's rotors into motion and the kinetic energy derived from it is used to generate electricity.

82 - Plumbing

Around 1700 BC, the Minoan Palace of Knossos on the isle of Crete had four separate drainage systems that emptied into great sewers constructed from stone. Terracotta pipes were laid below the palace floor, which could not be seen. Each section was about 2½ feet long, slightly tapered at one end and nearly one inch in diameter. It provided water for fountains and faucets of marble,

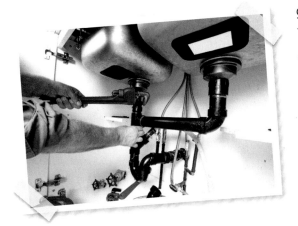

gold and silver that jetted hot and cold water. This is what we know as the first evidence of plumbing. Concealed in the palace latrine was the world's first flushing "water closet" or toilet, which had a wooden seat and a small reservoir of water. This device was lost for thousands of years. It was during the 16th century that Sir John Harington invented a "washout" closet, which was similar to the earlier one.

83 - Compass

The first compass was invented in China and it did not look much like the compasses that are in use today. A mineral called lodestone, which is composed largely of iron ore, was found to orient itself in the north-south direction no matter how it was kept. At first, this "stone compass" was used by fortune tellers.

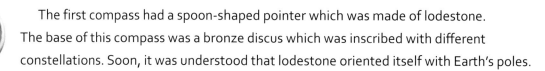

The first compass had a spoon-shaped pointer which was made of lodestone. The base of this compass was a bronze discus which was inscribed with different constellations. Soon, it was understood that lodestone oriented itself with Earth's poles.

The magnetised needle that we see in compasses today only appeared in the 11th century. The needle could be placed on water to make a wet compass. It could be placed on a pivot to make a dry compass. It could also be hung from a thread.

Compasses made it possible for people to travel further. Sailors from China managed to travel as far as the Middle East without getting lost. Today, magnets have become far more sophisticated. Magnetometers are even embedded in smartphones, which enable them to act as compasses.

84 Palanquin

A palanquin is a means of transport. It consists of a covered seating area that rests upon one or two horizontal poles. The poles are then hoisted upon the shoulders of the porters, who carry it around from one place to another.

The first mention of a palanquin comes from the Hindu epic text, the Mahabharata, which dates back to around 250 BC. However, different versions of the palanquin have existed before. The Bible mentions that the Ark of the Covenant, which was used to carry the commandments from God, was also carried in a palanquin-like structure.

85 Candles

Candles were among the earliest inventions, as shown by candlesticks from Egypt and Crete, that date back to at least 3000 BC. Evidence of candles in China can be seen by examining their metal furniture, which had prongs to hold candles. In India, candle wax was made by boiling cinnamon. Other sources of wax included insects, nuts and seeds.

One strange source of wax that was used in ancient times was the eulachon or candlefish. As this fish has very high levels of body fat, it could be dried and used as a candle!

Candles soon grew very popular because they quickly became an essential part of religious ceremonies. As candles burn at a relatively constant rate, they were also used to tell time.

86 Lever

Have you ever sat on a seesaw? If you have, you will know what a lever is. It consists of a beam and a fulcrum. When you apply force on one end, the other end is lifted up. It is easier to push down than to lift up, as when you do the former, the force of gravity also works with you. Thus, levers make the job of lifting easier.

It's impossible to gauge exactly when levers were invented. It is suspected that they were used in ancient Egypt to build pyramids. Greek inventor Archimedes also published laws that helped us understand the lever better.

87 Dome

A dome is a round, architectural structure that usually forms the roof of a building. Simple, dome-like structures have been seen throughout history. Prehistoric structures from 10,000 BC used mammoth tusks and bones to create a curved ceiling. An Inuit igloo also has a domed ceiling.

The Romans pioneered large-scale domes. These domes required strong base walls to hold them up. After the fall of the Roman Empire, the eastern Roman or Byzantine Empire carried the legacy forward. The Hagia Sophia is famous for its huge dome and still remains one of the greatest architectural wonders of the world.

88 Milling

Milling or grinding is the process of breaking food into finer particles so that it can be consumed easily. Milling also refers to separating, sizing or classifying any kind of material, for example, rock crushing or grinding to produce a uniform size of materials for construction purposes, separation of rock soil for the purpose of land fill or land reclamation activities.

The story behind the invention of milling may never be known to us, for there is no record of where it was first used. The very first type of grinding mill was a mortar and pestle. The grains were powdered by hand in a mortar and pestle. Soon after, milling required a working animal, i.e. a horse mill, or through a windmill or watermill. Today, mills are also powered by electricity.

89 Julian Calendar

The Julian calendar was introduced by Julius Caesar around 40 BC. It was commonly used till the late 1500s. Some countries like Greece and Russia used it till the early 1900s, and some Orthodox Churches continue to use it even today.

The Julian calendar has 365.25 days. This causes an error of 1 day in approximately 128 years. This approximation of 365.25 days is achieved by including 1 leap year every 4 years. The Julian calendar has 1 leap year every 3 years. Every year that is evenly divisible by 4 is a leap year. However, the Julian calendar also introduced an error of an additional day every 128 years. This was later fixed in the Gregorian calendar.

90 Oven

An oven is a thermally insulated chamber used to heat, bake or dry a substance and is most commonly used for cooking. The earliest ovens were found in Central Europe, dating back to 2900 BC. They were roasting and boiling pits. The first written historical record of an oven dates back to 1490 in Alsace, France. This oven was made of bricks and tiles.

Inventors began enhancing wood-burning ovens to contain the smoke they produced. Fire chambers were invented to contain the wood fire and holes were built into the top of these chambers so that cooking pots with flat bottoms could be placed directly on them. The 1735 "Castrol stove" or "stew stove" invented by French architect François Cuvilliés completely controlled the fire and had several openings covered by iron plates with holes.

Ovens were used by cultures that lived in the Indus Valley and pre-dynastic Egypt. By 3200 BC, each mud-brick house had an oven in settlements across the Indus Valley. Ovens were used to cook food and make bricks. Pre-dynastic civilisations in Egypt used kilns around 5000–4000 BC for pottery.

91 Postal Service

The origins of postal systems can be traced back to 2000 BC, in Egypt. During the sixth century BC, the Persian Empire, under the rule of Cyrus the Great, used a system of relay messengers.

In China, a post house service had been started by the Chou Dynasty. It was mostly used to convey official documents. This system had relays of couriers who changed horses at relay posts that were 14.5 km apart. The system flourished under the Han Empire from 202 BC to 220 AD, when the Chinese encountered the Romans and their postal system. The Roman system, known as "curcus publicus" was the most highly developed system in the ancient world. Their messengers were known to cover a distance of almost 270 km over a day and night!

92 Swimsuit

The first recorded use of a form of swimsuit dates back to Greece in 350 BC. The early 1800s witnessed a revolution with regards to the swimsuit when Americans would travel in groups to the beach for recreation. The first swimsuits consisted of bloomers and black stockings. By 1855, drawers were worn to avoid exposure when wearing the swimsuit. Improvements were made regarding the cut of the suit. By the 1880s, the "Princess" cut was introduced, consisting of a blouse and trousers in one piece. The skirts were replaced by cotton-like trousers. A separate skirt fell below the knee and buttoned at the waist to conceal the figure. A ruffled cap or a straw hat was also worn to complete the attire.

INSPIRATION

93 - Socks

Studies suggest that the first socks were made during the Stone Age using animal skins, which people tied around their ankles. By the eighth century BC, Greek poet Hesiod wrote about "piloi", which are socks made from matted animal hair. The Romans began wrapping their feet in strips of leather or woven fabric. By the second century AD, they were wearing "udones", which were sewn from woven fabric and pulled over one's foot. The first real knit socks were discovered in the Egyptian tombs between the third and sixth centuries. In Europe, socks were basically strips of cloth or hide that were wrapped around the legs and feet. They were called "leggings". 1938 saw the development of nylon, which led to the blending of two or more fabrics, a process that is currently used in the production of socks. Other fabrics such as acrylic, polyester, polyamide and spandex are also used.

The trend to produce colourful socks led to a major blend of new styles, patterns and looks. Coloured socks are often a part of school uniforms and are worn by sports teams on the field.

Socks are available in all shapes and sizes. There are knee-high socks, toe socks, short socks, anklets, over-the-knee socks, bare socks and more.

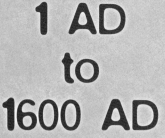

 **Paper**

Paper was first invented in China in 105 AD. It was invented by Cai Lun, an official at the Imperial court of the Han Dynasty during the early second century. Paper is a thin material that is produced by pressing together moist fibres such as cellulose pulp, which is obtained from wood, rags or grasses, and then dried to create sheets.

Paper is used in several ways. While its most common use is for writing and printing, it is also widely used as a packaging material, in many cleaning products, in a number of industrial and construction processes and even as a food ingredient, mainly in Asian cultures. The word paper is derived from "papyrus", which is the ancient Greek name of the "Cyprus papyrus" plant. Papyrus is a thick, paper-like material that is produced from the pith of the Cyprus papyrus plant, which was used in ancient Egypt and other Mediterranean cultures for writing, much before paper was invented.

The knowledge of papermaking moved from China to Japan, then to Korea in 610 AD, where it was commonly made from mulberry bark and Gampi (Japanese shrubs). Later, it was made from bamboo and rice straw.

95 Abacus

Abacus was developed by the Chinese and was used for calculations like addition, subtraction, multiplication and division as well as fractions and square roots.

A Chinese abacus has a wooden frame that is divided into two parts. These are separated by a beam with an upper deck of two rows of beads and a lower deck of five rows of beads. A series of vertical rods allows the wooden beads to slide freely. Traditionally, the abacus was made of wood or stone.

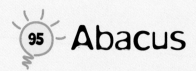

96 Toothbrush

The modern toothbrush was invented in 1938, much later than the toothpaste. Early forms of the toothbrush have existed since 3000 BC. Ancient civilisations used a thin twig with a frayed end to clean their teeth.

The bristle toothbrush, similar to the type used today, was not invented until 1498 in China. The stiff, coarse hair from the back of a pig's neck were used as bristles, attached to handles made of bone or bamboo.

Nylon bristles were introduced in 1938 by Dupont de Nemours. The first nylon toothbrush was called "Doctor West's Miracle Toothbrush".

97 Vault (Architecture)

A vault with regards to architecture is a structural aspect that consists of an arrangement of arches, usually forming a ceiling or roof. In ancient Egypt, brick vaulting was used for drains.

Vaults have various forms. The simplest form is the tunnel vault, also known as the barrel vault, which can be described as a "continuous arch". The weight of such a vault requires thick, supportive walls with limited gaps. As the height of a tunnel vault should increase along with its width, there is a practical limit to its size.

98 Hydrometer

A Greek scholar, Hypatia of Alexandria, has been given the credit for inventing the hydrometer during the late fourth century or early fifth century.

A hydrometer is an instrument that is used to measure the specific gravity or density of liquids. It is usually made of glass. It consists of a cylindrical stem and a bulb weighted with mercury or lead to make it float upright. The liquid to be tested is poured into a tall container, often a cylinder, and the hydrometer is gently lowered into the liquid until it floats freely. The point at which the surface of the liquid touches the stem of the hydrometer is noted. Hydrometers usually contain a scale inside the stem, so that the specific gravity can be read directly.

INSPIRATION

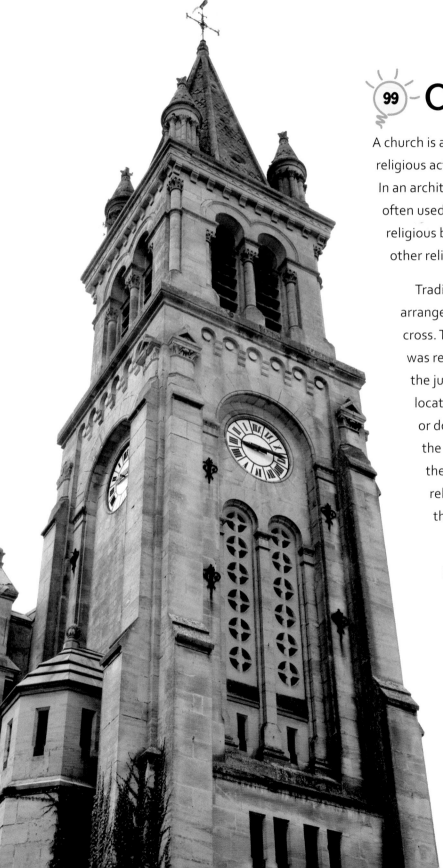

99 Church

A church is a building that is used for religious activities, particularly worship. In an architectural sense, the term is often used by Christians to refer to their religious buildings, but can be used by other religions also.

Traditionally, a church was often arranged in the shape of a Christian cross. The longest part of the cross was represented by the aisle and the junction of the cross was located at the altar area. Towers or domes were added so that the viewer could look towards the heavens, thereby inspiring religious devotees who visited the church.

Modern church buildings have a variety of architectural styles and layouts. The earliest identified Christian church was founded between 233 and 256.

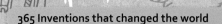

(100) Paper Money

The first recorded use of paper money was believed to be in China during the seventh century. The Chinese used paper currency to avoid carrying heavy and cumbersome metallic coins for transactions. Similar to making a deposit at a modern bank, individuals would transfer their coins to a trustworthy party and then receive a note denoting how much money they had deposited. The note could then be redeemed for currency at a later date. They continued this process for more than 500 years before the practice spread to Europe in the 17th century.

(101) Cannon

The cannon was first invented in China and is among the earliest forms of gunpowder artillery. In the Middle East, it is debated that the hand cannon was first used during the Battle of Ain Jalut between the Mamluks and Mongols in 1260. The first cannon in Europe was probably used in Iberia during the 11th and 12th centuries.

The word cannon is derived from the old Italian word "cannone", which means a "large tube". It has a truncated cone with an internal, cylindrical bore for holding an explosive charge and a projectile.

The world's earliest known cannon dates back to 1282 and was found in Mongol-held Manchuria.

102 Pretzel

In 610, while baking bread, an Italian monk decided to create a treat to motivate his distracted catechism students. He rolled out ropes of dough and twisted them so that they looked like hands crossed on the chest in prayer, and he baked them. The monk called his snacks "pretiola", which is Latin for "little reward". When the pretiola arrived in Germany, it was called "brezel". Because of its religious roots, the pretzel has long been considered a good-luck symbol. German children wear pretzels around their necks on New Year's Day. The pretzel serves as an emblem for bakers since the 12th century.

Pretzels now have different shapes. Salt is the most common seasoning for pretzels, complementing the washing soda or lye treatment that gives pretzels their traditional "skin" and flavour through the Maillard reaction. Other seasonings include sugars, chocolate, glazes, seeds and/or nuts.

Pretzels were regarded as having religious significance for both ingredients and shape in the Catholic Church. Pretzels made with a simple recipe of only flour and water could be eaten during Lent, when Christians were forbidden to eat eggs, lard or dairy products such as milk and butter. With time, pretzels were associated with both Lent and Easter. Pretzels were hidden on Easter morning just as eggs are hidden today and are particularly associated with Lent, fasting and prayers before Easter.

103 - Gun

The first recorded gun firing
occurred in China during the 13th
century. The first firearm was the
fire lance, the prototype of a gun. The fire
lance was invented in China during the 10th century. The term
"gun" may refer to any sort of projectile weapon ranging from large
cannons to small firearms, including those that are handheld.
A gun is a normally tubular weapon or any other device designed to discharge
projectiles or other materials.

Guns are used for self-defence. However, they have been misused for a long time. To own a gun, one must have a licence. Today, several types of guns are available around the world.

104 - Gunpowder

Ancient Chinese alchemists were trying to find a formula for immortality and ended up creating gunpowder. It was a mixture of sulphur, saltpetre (potassium nitrate) and charcoal. When the Chinese found out that it exploded, they began to use it for fireworks. After a few hundred years, they started using it for war. They first used it at the beginning of a war to try and scare the people who fought them. The Chinese realised that if you explode gunpowder near people, they might die, so they started using it in wars as an explosive.

In the 12th and 13th centuries,
gunpowder spread to the Arab
countries, then Greece, other
European countries and finally
all over the world.

105 Velvet

Velvet is a woven fabric in which the cut threads are evenly distributed. It has a short, dense pile that gives it a unique feel. Velvet can be made from synthetic or natural fibres. This fabric originated in Kashmir. It is associated with nobility. Velvet is woven on a special loom that simultaneously weaves two thicknesses of the material. The weaving technique dates back to as early as 2000 BC in Egypt. Because of its fairly intricate manufacturing process, velvet was an extremely expensive fabric and continues to be fairly expensive even today.

106 Rocket

The first rocket was invented around 1100 AD in China. These rockets were mainly used as weapons and fireworks. It was during the 1920s that rocket societies emerged. By the 1930s and 1940s, professional rocket engineering began. Three pioneers began working independently on developing rockets to reach space. Konstantin Tsiolkovsky and Hermann Oberth were the first to come up with many essential principles and realise that the rocket could be used as a means to travel into space. This created a curiosity about rocketry and space travel. In 1926, Robert Goddard launched the first liquid-propellant rocket. Due to its secrecy, the 1926 rocket did not influence later developments.

(107) Dress

It is not known who invented the dress or when they invented it. It cannot be credited to a single inventor.

Women often wore tunics overlaid with fabrics in ancient societies, right up to the Middle Ages. Back then, wearing fabric became a way for nobility to showcase their status in society. By adding more fabric to tunics, females could show off their position in society. This led to the evolution of dresses. The tunic was gradually reduced to being peasant-wear and gowns became the symbol of high society. Clothing became so important during the Middle Ages that laws were passed about the types of clothing that people of various social strata could and could not wear.

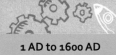

108 Spinning Wheel

The spinning wheel has been in use since ancient times when spinning was done on a spindle. The spindle was a stick with a stone or some weight attached to it. The earliest evidence of a spinning wheel comes from Baghdad in 1234, China around 1270 and Europe around 1280. Evidence suggests that spinning wheels were used in both China and the Islamic world during the 11th century. According to Irfan Habib, the spinning wheel was introduced in India from Iran in the 13th century. In France, the spinning wheel was not used until the mid-18th century.

To use a spinning wheel, cleaned wool or cotton is first carded. This means that cotton is spread on one card and combed with another, until the fibres are all facing one direction. The carding is done with hand cards and coarse nail brushes that are about 12 inches long and five inches wide. The cotton is then twisted loosely and finally spun into yarn. It is then taken off in fleecy rolls that are about 12 inches long and three quarters of an inch thick. These short cardings are twisted on the spinning wheel into a loose thread, about the size of a candlewick. These threads are wound on reels or bobbins and finally spun into the finished yarn. Several types of fibres can be spun on a simple spinning wheel.

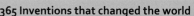

109 Rifle

Rifled firearms date back to the 15th century Europe. In 1610, artist, gunsmith and inventor Marin le Bourgeoys developed the first "flintlock" for King Louis XIII of France. A rifle is a firearm that is designed to be fired from the shoulder. It has a barrel with a helical groove or a pattern of grooves cut into the barrel walls. The trigger releases a spring-loaded mechanism that causes a flint to strike a steel surface. The spark ignites gunpowder and propels a spherical bullet.

Formerly, rifles only fired a single projectile with each squeeze of the trigger. Modern rifles are capable of firing more than one round per trigger squeeze. Some are fully automatic and others are limited to fixed bursts of two, three or more rounds per squeeze.

110 Lace

Lace is a delicate, openwork fabric made of yarn or thread, often found on fancy attire. It is patterned with open holes in the work, which can be made by machine or hand. The holes can be formed by removing threads or pieces of cloth from a previously woven fabric, but more often, these open spaces are created as a part of the lace fabric.

Lacemaking is an ancient craft that can be traced all the way back to the early 16th century. While many have debated over the inventor of lace, it is hard to give the credit to one person as lacemaking evolved from various other techniques. Lace gained a lot of popularity during the 1500s, when it started to make an appearance in both fashion and home decor.

Open woven fabrics and fine nets that had a lace-like effect are known to have existed for centuries. Originally, lace was created using linen, silk, gold or silver threads. Today, lace is often made with cotton thread.

111 Spectacles

Evidence suggests that glasses first appeared in Pisa, Italy, around 1268. They were formed from two simple convex-shaped glass/crystal stones. Each of these was surrounded by a frame and given a handle. These were connected together through the ends of their handles by a rivet. They were not an invention, but an idea based on the simple glass stone magnifier. Someone took two, existing, mounted stones and connected them with a rivet. The first pair of glasses was invented by a lay person who wanted to keep the process a secret in order to make a profit. Spectacles are used to correct your vision if you cannot clearly see things that are at a distance or even nearby.

Though the eyeglasses existed for a while, it was troublesome to keep them on the eye. Finally, in 1730, an optician named Edward Scarlett found a solution to keeping them on by using rigid side pieces that could be hooked behind the ears.

Today, glasses are available in many types, based on their primary function, but they also appear in combinations such as prescription sunglasses or safety glasses that enhance magnification.

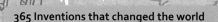
112 - Screwdriver

The inventor of the screw is unknown, although screw-shaped tools were a common item since the first century. The first screwdrivers were used to unscrew corks on wine and olive oil bottles. Initially, they were made of wood, but now they are made of metal for extra strength, durability and stability. To accompany the screwdriver, metal screws and nuts were created to fasten two objects together in the 15th century. The screwdriver was designed to insert and tighten bolts or screws, or loosen and remove bolts or screws.

113 - Electricity

Electricity was never invented because it is a form of energy that occurs naturally. Rubbing amber on a cat's fur attracted light objects. This was known to ancient cultures around the Mediterranean. Around 600 BC, Thales of Miletus became the earliest researcher of electricity. He rubbed fur with other objects and found them to attract each other. What he actually discovered was "static electricity".

In 1600, English physician William Gilbert studied the relationship between electricity and magnetism in detail. He was able to find the lodestone effect due to static electricity, which was produced by rubbing amber. Gilbert named it after the Latin word "electricus", meaning "of amber". He is said to be the father of modern electricity. In 1646, Thomas Browne's "Pseudodoxia Epidemica" included the English words "electric" and "electricity".

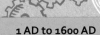

114 · Pencil

Pencils were first produced in the 16th century. A large deposit of graphite was discovered in Borrowdale, England, during the first half of the 1500s. Local residents cut the graphite into sticks and used them to mark their sheep. The graphite was misidentified as lead, a word that has been connected with pencils ever since, even though modern pencils do not contain lead. Graphite left a darker mark than lead, but it was soft and brittle, so it had to be held. Therefore, it was inserted into hollow, wooden sticks.

Later, an Italian couple, Simonio and Lyndiana Bernacotti, invented the pencil in its modern form around 1560. They hollowed out a stick of juniper wood and placed a graphite stick inside. Another technique was developed where a graphite stick was inserted into two wooden halves that were glued together. This basic technique remained in use even 400 years later.

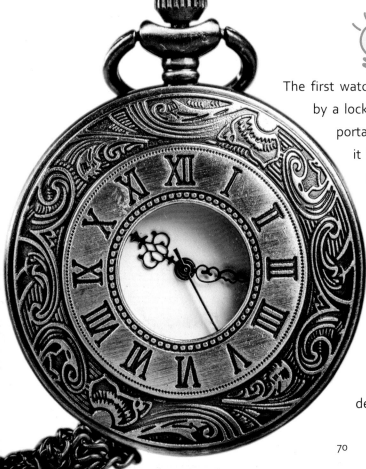

115 · Watch

The first watch was invented in the 1500s in Germany by a locksmith named Peter Hanlein. It was like a portable clock. However, it was so heavy that it had to be held by a belt, which was worn around the waist.

A watch is a mechanical device, which is powered by winding a main spring. This spring turns the gears that are responsible for moving the hands. These hands keep account of time with a rotating balance wheel.

The history of the watch spans 500 years, of which, most of the time was devoted to refining the mechanical watch.

116 Printing Press

A printing press is a machine which evenly prints ink on paper or cloth. Typically used for texts, the invention and spread of the printing press is widely regarded as one of the most influential events in human history. It is said to have originated around the second century, when the Chinese used wooden blocks to "press" images of flowers on silk. The first printing press was operated by hand.

In 1440, a German inventor named Johannes Gutenberg invented a process that allowed the printing of multiple books at a time. While this technique was refined and enhanced over the years, it continued to be the principal means of printing until the late 20th century.

During the 19th century, other inventors created steam powered printing presses that did not require a hand operator. Today's printing presses are electronic and automated, and can print faster than their earlier versions.

The printing press is one of the most important inventions in history. It has ensured that books, newspapers, magazines and other reading materials are produced in great numbers. It plays an important role in promoting literacy among people.

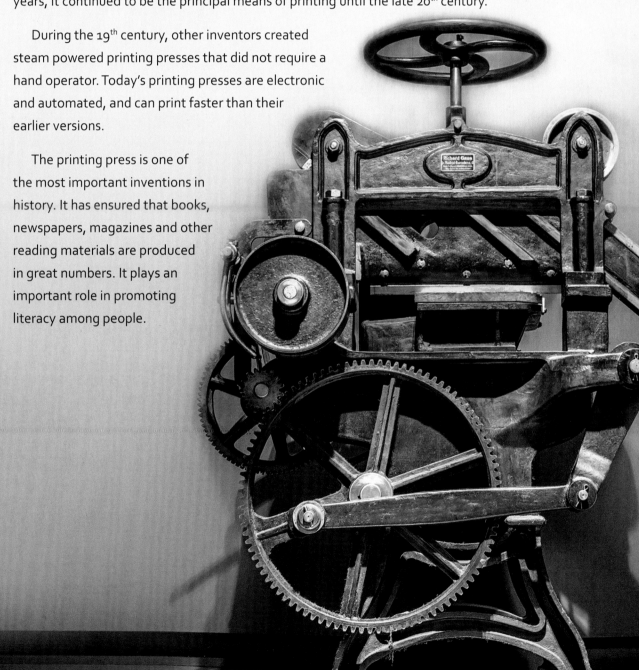

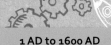

INSPIRATION

117 - Corset

A corset is a close-fitting, stiff piece of clothing that provides shape to a woman's torso. It was a popular garment during the 16th century. However, the term "corset" was used from the 19th century. Prior to that, the corset was called "bodies", "a stiff bodice" or "a pair of stays".

The first corset was invented during 1500–1550. It was made from stiff materials like whalebone, horn and buckram, and was referred to as "whalebone bodies". A stay is placed vertically in the centre of the torso to keep it straight.

French queen Catherine de Medici, wife of King Henry II, introduced the corset to France.

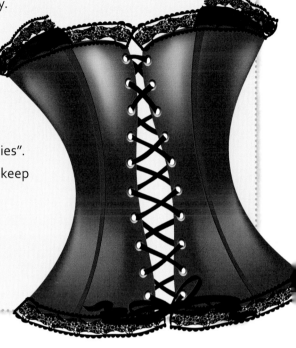

118 - Teapot

The teapot was invented in the 1500s by clay potters in the Yixing Province of China during the Ming Dynasty period. Initially, teapots were small, unglazed brown or red pieces of pottery with wide bases, spouts and handles, and were used exclusively for brewing tea. These pots were able to withstand extreme heat when hot, boiling liquids were poured into them. In the 1600s, teapots were brought by Dutch importers from China to Europe along with chests of tea leaves. After a century of experimentation, European potters finally managed to produce a quality teapot similar to the heat-resistant Chinese ones.

Since then, the teapot has evolved from plain clay to fine glazed porcelain and to translucent and exquisite bone China. In spite of these new varieties, authentic Yixing teapots continue to be highly coveted by tea enthusiasts.

(119) Microscope

During the 1590s, two Dutch spectacle makers, Zacharias Jansen and his father Hans, started experimenting with glass lenses. They put several lenses in a tube that led to a very important discovery. The object near the end of the tube appeared to be greatly enlarged, much larger than any simple magnifying glass could achieve by itself.

Their first microscopes were more of a novelty and not very useful, since the maximum magnification was only around 9x (times) and the images were blurry to a certain extent. The early Jansen microscopes were compound and used a minimum of two lenses. The objective lens was positioned close to the object. It produced an image that was picked up and magnified further by the second lens, which was called the "eyepiece".

Antony van Leeuwenhoek was the first man to make and use the modern microscope. Leeuwenhoek ground and polished a small glass ball into a lens with a magnification of 270x, and used this lens to make the microscope.

Because it had only one lens, his microscope is now commonly referred to as a single-lens microscope. Its convex glass lens was attached to a metal holder and focused with the help of screws. Leeuwenhoek constructed a total of 400 microscopes during his prolific lifetime.

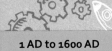

120 - Heeled Shoes

High-heeled shoes were first worn by men! They were used in the 16th century by Persian soldiers who rode on horseback. The shoes offered stability in the stirrups to the soldiers so they could use their bow and arrows more efficiently. Later, in 17th century Europe, they caught on as a fashion statement for the aristocracy. Around the 1630s, women started adopting masculine fashion trends and began wearing high heels.

The year 1533 saw the first women's heel that was designed to lengthen the legs. The invention of high heels as a fashion statement could be accredited to the rather petite Catherine de Medici. Heels were adopted by the European aristocracy during the 1600s as a sign of status.

121 - Stockings

Stockings are also known as hosiery, hose and popularly as "nylons". They are used as a covering for legs and feet. Early references to stockings date back to the ancient Greeks. Workmen and slaves wore hosiery in ancient times, and Roman women wore a short sock called a "soccus" within their homes. Silk or cotton stockings were also worn in Japan and China for centuries.

The soccus evolved into stockings in 12th century Europe. After 1545, knitted stockings came into fashion. Interestingly, several pairs of silk stockings were sometimes worn during winter, even though knitted stockings offered more warmth!

122 · Bullet

A bullet is a projectile (often pointed) metal cylinder that is shot from a firearm. After 1249, it was understood that gunpowder could be used to fire projectiles out of the open end of a tube. The earliest firearms were large cannons, but small and personal firearms appeared only in the mid-14th century. Early projectiles were stone or metal objects that could fit down the barrel of the firearm. Lead and lead alloys came to be used by 1550.

Bullet is usually a part of an ammunition cartridge, the object that contains the bullet. It is inserted into the firearm. Bullets are made from a variety of materials. Lead or a lead alloy is the traditional bullet core material. There are many other materials that are used in bullets today, including aluminium, bismuth, bronze, copper, plastics, rubber, steel, tin and tungsten.

123 · Hats

Hats have been around for a long time. They were used for protection and as a fashionable accessory. Additionally, they are known to have a long history as markers of status, occupation and even political affiliation.

One of the first hats to be depicted was found in a tomb painting at "Thebes". It showed a man wearing a coolie-style straw hat. In the late 17th century, women's headgear rose to fame. Women's hats were starkly different from the ones that men wore around that time.

A maker of women's hats was called a "milliner". This term dates back to 1529. It referred to the products that made Milan and northern Italian regions famous.

124 Clothes Iron

Various objects have been used for centuries to remove wrinkles and press clothing. However, there was a time when this could only be afforded by rich people. Slaves or servants were hired to do the work. Around 400 BC, the Greeks used a "goffering" iron to create pleats on linen robes. The goffering iron was a round bar that was heated before use.

By the 10th century, Vikings from Scandinavia had early irons made of glass. They used a linen smoother to iron pleats. This smoother was warmed by being held near steam and then rubbed across the fabric. The iron first appeared in Europe in the 1300s. It constituted a flat piece of iron with a metal handle and was held over a fire till it turned hot.

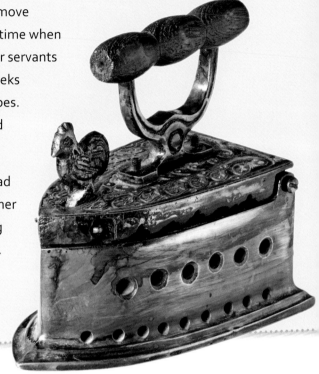

125 Gregorian Calendar

The calendar that we refer to today is the Gregorian calendar. It was proposed by Aloysius Lilius, a physician from Naples and was adopted by Pope Gregory XIII to correct the errors in the older Julian calendar. This calendar was officially declared by Pope Gregory XIII in 1582.

In the Gregorian calendar, the tropical year is approximated as 36597/400 days = 365.2425 days. Therefore, it takes approximately 3,300 years for the tropical year to shift one day with respect to the Gregorian calendar. The approximation 36597/400 is achieved by having 97 leap years in every 400 years.

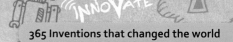

126 - Thermometer

Thermometers are used to measure temperature. This is carried out using materials that change in a particular manner when heated or cooled. In a mercury or alcohol thermometer, the liquid expands when it is heated and contracts when it is cooled. Before the thermometer, an instrument called the thermoscope was used. It was a thermometer without a scale. A thermoscope only showed the differences in temperatures. For example, it could show that something was getting hotter.

Several inventors simultaneously invented various versions of the thermoscope. In 1592, Galileo Galilei invented a simple water thermoscope, which enabled different temperatures to be measured. Today, Galileo's invention is called the "Galileo Thermometer".

In 1612, an Italian inventor named Santorio Santorio became the first inventor to put a numerical scale on his thermoscope. It was the first, basic, clinical thermometer, as it was designed to be placed in a patient's mouth for checking the temperature. In 1654, the first, enclosed thermometer was invented by Duke Ferdinand II of Tuscany. He used alcohol in it. However, it was still inaccurate and did not use a standardised scale. Daniel Gabriel Fahrenheit invented the first mercury thermometer with a standardised scale in 1714.

1601 AD to 1800 AD

127 Railroad

"Wagonways" were the first railroads that came into existence. They were used in Germany in 1550. These railed roads comprised wooden rails over which horse drawn wagons or carts moved with greater ease as compared to dirt roads. Wagonways paved the start of modern railroads.

By 1776, the wooden rails and wheels on the carts were replaced by iron. Wagonways evolved into tramways and spread throughout Europe. Even then, horses were used to pull these carts. In 1789, Englishman William Jessup created the first wagon with flanged wheels. The flange was a groove that allowed the wheels to have a better grip on the rail. This was a beneficial design that aided the later versions of locomotives.

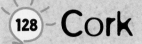

128 Cork

One does not know exactly when humans thought about using the bark of a tree to plug a bottle. The material used to make the cork is found on the bark of the cork oak tree. It is made from dead cells that accumulate on the outer surface. Cork bottle stoppers were found in Egyptian tombs that were thousands of years old. Ancient Greeks used corks to make fishing net floats, sandals and bottle stoppers. Romans used corks for various purposes, including life jackets for fishermen. For centuries, Mediterranean cottages have been built with cork roofs and floors to prevent them from getting too hot or cold.

A cork tree can be harvested when it is around 20 years old. The use of cork as a stopper grew wildly popular, leading to an increase in the cultivation of cork trees.

129 Bowtie

Bowties came to be worn since the 1700s. Earlier, Europeans wore scarves around their necks to hold the tops of their shirts in place at the collar. The black bow tie being a part of the "black tie" attire was first used in 1886, when the tuxedo was invented by Pierre Lorillard V. Earlier, the fashion was to wear tailcoats with white bow ties. The tuxedo is one such attire that has survived all eras and the only accurate complement to such a suit is the bowtie.

130 - Submarine

Sketches of a submarine were first created by Leonardo da Vinci. In 1578, William Bourne, a British mathematician, drew plans for a submarine. However, the first submarine was created in 1620 by Cornelius van Drebbel, a Dutch inventor. He tightly wrapped a wooden rowboat in waterproofed leather and added air tubes with floats to the surface to provide oxygen. His submarine had no engines, so the oars went through the hull at leather gaskets.

The first submarine to be used for military purposes was built in 1775 by American inventor David Bushnell. His submarine was a one-man, wooden submarine that was powered by hand-turned propellers.

Two American inventors, John P. Holland and Simon Lake, developed the first true submarines in the 1890s. The US Navy purchased submarines built by Holland, while Russia and Japan chose Lake's designs. Their submarines used petrol or steam engines for surface cruising and electric motors underwater. The first nuclear-powered submarine, the "USS Nautilus", was launched in 1954.

131 - Steam Engine

Thomas Savery was the first to invent a steam pump in 1698. He called it "water by fire". In 1712, Thomas Newcomen invented an effective and practical steam engine. It consisted of a piston or cylinder that moved a huge piece of wood to drive the water pump. This engine was used for more than 50 years.

The invention of the steam engine was a difficult process. Three different British inventors took about 100 years to develop it. In September 1825, the Stockton & Darlington Railroad Company was the first railroad to carry both goods and passengers on regular schedules using locomotives designed by English inventor George Stephenson. It pulled six loaded coal cars and 21 passenger cars with 450 passengers over 14 km in about one hour.

George Stephenson is considered to be the inventor of the first steam locomotive engine.

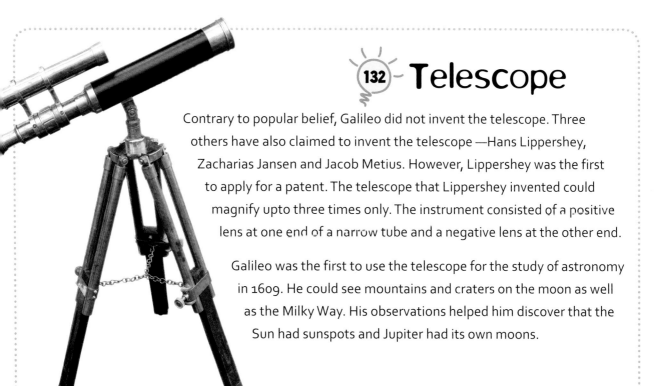

132 Telescope

Contrary to popular belief, Galileo did not invent the telescope. Three others have also claimed to invent the telescope —Hans Lippershey, Zacharias Jansen and Jacob Metius. However, Lippershey was the first to apply for a patent. The telescope that Lippershey invented could magnify upto three times only. The instrument consisted of a positive lens at one end of a narrow tube and a negative lens at the other end.

Galileo was the first to use the telescope for the study of astronomy in 1609. He could see mountains and craters on the moon as well as the Milky Way. His observations helped him discover that the Sun had sunspots and Jupiter had its own moons.

133 - Tie

A necktie or tie is a long piece of cloth that is worn around the neck or shoulders. It rests under the shirt collar and is knotted in the front of the neck. A tie is worn for style.

The actual year of invention of the tie is debatable. It is believed that the tie was first used by Croatian soldiers during the Thirty Year War that started in the 1600s. The word "cravatte" was used to describe the handkerchief that Croatian soldiers tied around their necks during the war. This made it easy to identify them. Silk ties were strictly reserved for officers, while the soldiers wore ties of ordinary materials.

King Louis XVI of France began sporting a lace cravatte during 1646, when he was just seven years old. This set the trend of neckties among the French nobility of that era. It was only during the period of 1910 to 1919 that neckties began to resemble the modern ones we see today.

134 - Barometer

The word barometer is derived from the Greek words "baros", which means weight and "metron", which means measure. The barometer is used to measure air pressure. Barometer uses the principal of a vacuum to measure the weight of air.

The first working barometer was created in 1643 by Evangelista Torricelli. He worked with and studied the writings of Galileo, just before Galileo's untimely death in 1642.Torricelli used those findings to construct the first barometer, which made use of water to measure the air pressure during that time.

135 Blood Transfusion

Blood transfusion is the process of receiving blood products directly into your blood stream through your veins. Transfusions are used for various medically-associated conditions to replace lost components of blood. Early transfusions used whole blood, but modern medical practice only uses components of blood, such as red blood cells, white blood cells, plasma, clotting factors and platelets.

The first research on blood transfusion dates back to the 17th century when British physician William Harvey described the circulation and properties of blood in 1628. The first blood transfusions were also tried during this period, but they often failed and proved dangerous to humans.

The first successful blood transfusion was performed by British physician Richard Lower in 1665. He let a dog almost bleed to death and revived it by transfusing blood from another dog through a tied artery. In 1667, Jean-Baptiste Denis, King Louis XIV's physician, performed blood transfusion from an animal to a human. He transfused blood from a sheep to a 15-year old boy and later to a labourer. Both these transfusions were successful.

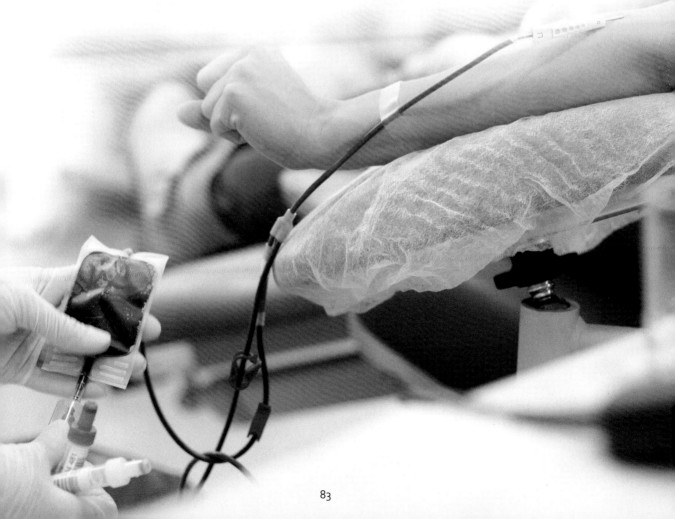

136 Parachute

The first time someone thought of an idea similar to a parachute was in 1514, when Leonardo da Vinci sketched its design in his notebook. Many years later, another man by the name of Fausto Veranzio published his own design, which was strikingly similar to that of Da Vinci. Veranzio went on to explain exactly how this device worked by jumping from a high place, because he believed that it would work. However, the first man to successfully try the parachute is said to be a French man named J.P. Blanchard. He dropped a little dog sitting in a basket all by itself from a hot air balloon in flight and watched it safely land on the ground. He even claimed that he used the parachute himself in 1793, but broke his leg when he touched the ground.

The first man to use the parachute regularly and on recorded documentation was another Frenchman named André Jacques Garnerin. The first time that he went parachuting was in 1797, when he jumped off a height of 600 m but landed safely and securely.

(137) Refrigerator

Oliver Evans first invented the refrigerator in 1805. However, William Cullen invented the process in 1748 and Jacob Perkins added improvements to the refrigerator in 1834. The first refrigerator was introduced in 1834. By 1880, there were over 3,000 patents for refrigerators.

Albert Einstein also patented an invention of the refrigerator. In 1903, he invented an eco-friendly refrigerator, with no moving parts, that did not use electricity.

Earlier, people used iceboxes to keep their food cool and prevent it from getting spoilt. Iceboxes were lined with metal and insulated with straw, sawdust or cork. Blocks of ice were put on top so that cold air would circulate downwards to keep the food cool. A tap would be used to drain the melting water.

(138) Water Frame

Richard Arkwright was a barber and wig maker in Bolton around 1750. He learnt that he would become rich if he could invent a machine that would spin cotton fibre into yarn quickly and easily. He teamed up with a clockmaker named John Kay. By the late 1760s, they had a workable machine that spun four strands of cotton yarn at the same time. Arkwright patented this machine in 1769 to stop others from copying his invention.

The water frame spins 96 strands of yarn together. It was similar to the machines installed in the mills in Derbyshire and Lancashire that were powered by water wheels. As a result, they were called "Water Frames". Currently, it is the only machine of its kind in the world that is complete. Arkwright's machines did not require skilled operators.

139 Razor

During prehistoric times, clam shells or flint were used for removing hair. Later, between 3000 BC and 6000 BC, razors evolved from clam shells and flint to a more sophisticated device. Archaeologists discovered circular razors made of bronze in ancient Egyptian burial chambers.

The first safety razor was conceptualised around 1770 by Frenchman Jean-Jacques Perret. It consisted of a sharpened, straight razor with a wooden guard. During this period, shaving was done by professional barbers.

During 1895, a salesman named King C. Gillette came up with an idea for a double edged safety razor that would be made of cheap, disposable blades, which would not have to be sharpened. He was inspired by his colleague, William Painter, who suggested that one way to make money was to produce something cheap that people would need to buy repeatedly. However, it was difficult to mass produce such blades. In 1901, Gillette used the help of MIT graduate William Nickerson and by 1903, they had successfully invented a thin, sharp blade which could be produced in large quantities.

140 Mayonnaise

Some culinary historians observed that a mayonnaise-like mixture of olive oil and egg was frequently consumed by ancient Egyptians and Romans. The mayonnaise that we have today is an emulsion of oil, egg, lemon juice and/or vinegar along with different types of seasonings. This was developed by a chef from France.

Mayonnaise was invented by Duke de Richelieu's chef in 1756. When the Duke conquered a Mediterranean island, the chef wanted to prepare a victory sauce but lacked the essential ingredient - cream. So, he created a new sauce using eggs and olive oil, and named it "mahonnaise".

The first ready mayonnaise was sold at Richard Hellman's New York deli in 1905. In 1912, it was marketed and called "Hellman's Blue Ribbon Mayonnaise".

(141) Accelerometer

An accelerometer is used to measure different kinds of acceleration, i.e., the rate at which velocity changes. It was initially used to validate the principles of Newtonian physics.

The first accelerometer was invented by an English physicist George Atwood in 1783. It measured linear acceleration: for e.g., the rate at which an object falls. A spring system is used to measure the accelerating force, which provides acceleration using Newton's famous second law, i.e., force equals mass times acceleration. Later, accelerometers were designed to measure circular or twisting acceleration, like that of a weight attached at the end of a string. Here, the acceleration depends on the radius of the circle of the spinning object.

(142) Carbonated Water

Carbonated water, also known as club soda, soda water, sparkling water, seltzer water or fizzy water is water into which carbon dioxide gas has been dissolved under pressure. The first drinkable man-made glass of carbonated water was invented by Joseph Priestley in 1767.

In the late 18th century, J. J. Schweppe developed a process to manufacture carbonated mineral water using the same process discovered by Joseph Priestley, thus founding the Schweppes Company in Geneva in 1783. In 1799, Augustine Thwaites founded Thwaites' Soda Water in Dublin. Today, carbonated water is made by passing pressurised carbon dioxide through flavoured or regular water.

 143 Spinning Jenny

James Hargreaves invented a device to spin cotton in 1764. He named his invention the "Spinning Jenny" after his wife. This invention was important as it was the first improvement on the spinning wheel. It paved the way for the Industrial Revolution, which led people to leave the countryside and move to major cities. Therefore, it may be said that Hargreaves influenced European and eventually American lifestyles. His invention led to the setting up of textile mills all across Europe and even the USA.

Originally, the spinning jenny used eight spindles instead of the single one that was used on the spinning wheel. A single wheel on the spinning jenny controlled eight spindles, which created a weave using eight threads that were spun from a corresponding set of rovings. Later models had up to 120 spindles.

On 12 July, 1770, Hargreaves patented a 16-spindle spinning jenny. His invention decreased the need for labour. The only drawback was that his machine produced thread that was too thick to be used for warp threads and could only be used for weft threads.

(144) Sandwich

The first sandwich was said to be eaten during the first century BC by Hillel the Elder, a well-known rabbi. He began the Passover custom of sandwiching a mixture of chopped nuts, apples, spices and wine betweten two matzos, which was to be eaten along with bitter herbs. The filling between the matzos was a reminder of the suffering of the Jewish community before their deliverance from Egypt. It also represented the mortar that was used by the community during a period of forced labour while constructing Egyptian buildings. Because he was the first known person to do this and because of his influence and status in Palestinian Judaism, this practice was added to the Seder and the Hillel Sandwich was named after him.

Food historians attribute the conception of the sandwich to John Montagu, the fourth Earl of Sandwich. Montagu was an avid gambler. It is said that on 3 November, 1762, during a 24-hour gambling streak, he instructed a cook to prepare food in a manner that would not require him to stop playing his ongoing game. The cook offered him sliced meat that was placed between two pieces of toast. This meal did not need any utensils and could be eaten using only one hand, which left the other hand free to continue the game. While the Earl got credited for the invention, the name of his cook remains unknown.

145 Smallpox Vaccine

In 1788, scientist Edward Jenner inoculated a healthy, 8-year-old boy with cowpox. It is a disease that is caused by a virus closely resembling variola. Cowpox usually affects small mammals such as wood mice, but the virus can spread to other animals as well, especially cattle.

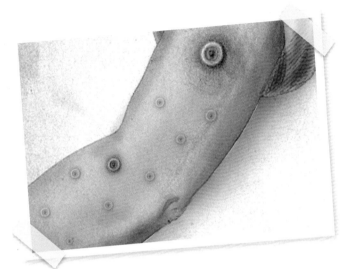

Jenner's experiment was successful. His patient did not contract smallpox, even when he was deliberately exposed to variola. By 1800, smallpox vaccinations were common, mainly because they caused fewer side effects and deaths than variolation with smallpox itself.

Smallpox vaccine was used in the USA until 1972.

 146 Steam Boat

Marquis Joffroy D'abans, a Frenchman, was the first to attempt to build a steam boat. He launched his steam boat in 1776 and called it "Palmipède". He placed a small, wood-fired steam engine on a river boat. The engine's rocker arms were connected to paddles that looked like duck feet when flopping in water. He attempted to sail it along the river Seine in Paris, but the boat did not move.

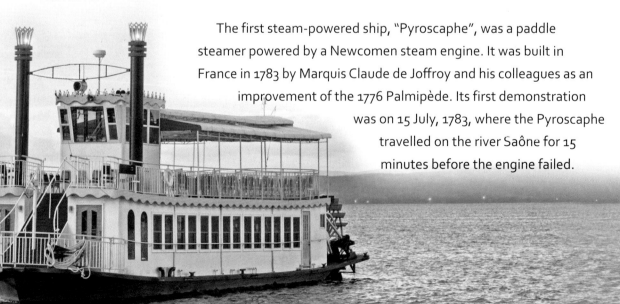

The first steam-powered ship, "Pyroscaphe", was a paddle steamer powered by a Newcomen steam engine. It was built in France in 1783 by Marquis Claude de Joffroy and his colleagues as an improvement of the 1776 Palmipède. Its first demonstration was on 15 July, 1783, where the Pyroscaphe travelled on the river Saône for 15 minutes before the engine failed.

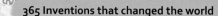

147 Iron Bridge

Abraham Darby cast the world's first iron bridge in
Coalbrookdale. He was a local ironmaster and his bridge was erected
across the River Severn in 1779. Shrewsbury architect, Thomas Pritchard first
suggested to ironmaster John Wilkinson in 1773 that an iron bridge should be built over
the Severn. Pritchard designed the bridge. The construction was completed in 1779. The
world's first iron bridge was opened on New Year's Day in 1781. It cost over £6,000.

The bridge is built from five cast iron ribs spanning across 30.6 metres or 100 feet. 378 tonnes
of iron were used to construct the bridge. Almost 1,700 individual components were used for
the construction, the heaviest weighing 5.5 tonnes. Individual components were cast to fit each
other instead of following standard sizes. There were discrepancies of up to several centimetres
between those components that were identical in different locations. The opening of the bridge
resulted in several changes in lifestyle for those living in the settlement. The condition of the
roads around the bridge improved in the years after its construction.

148 Hot Air Balloon

On 4 June, 1783, the Montgolfier brothers built a balloon made of silk and lined with paper that was 10 metres in diameter. They launched this giant balloon from the marketplace in Annonay, France. During their first attempt, nobody was aboard this balloon. It rose to a magnificent height of 1,600-2,000 metres and stayed aloft for 10 minutes. It travelled for a distance of about 2 km.

The Montgolfier brothers' next step was to put a person in the basket and fly it once again. On 15 October, 1783, they launched a balloon on a tether with Jean-François Pilâtre de Rozier, a chemistry and physics teacher, aboard. He stayed up in the air for almost four minutes.

About a month later, on 21st November, Pilâtre de Rozier and Marquis d'Arlandes, a French military officer, made the first free ascent in a hot air balloon. They flew from the middle of Paris all the way to the suburbs. They covered what was then considered an impressive distance of about 9 km in 25 minutes.

The next major point in balloon history was on 7 January, 1793. Jean Pierre Blanchard became the first man to fly a hot air balloon in North America, with George Washington's presence at the launch.

149 Thresher

Thresher was first invented by Scottish mechanical engineer Andrew Meikle around 1784 to separate grain from stalks and husks. For thousands of years, grain was separated by hand with flails, which was very difficult and time-consuming.

Early threshing machines were hand-fed and powered by horses. They were small, about the size of an upright piano. The later versions were steam-powered, driven by a portable or traction engine.

150 Cotton Gin

Eli Whitney invented a simple machine that influenced the history of the USA in 1793. He invented a cotton gin that was particularly popular in Southern states. The South became the cotton producing part of the country because Whitney's cotton gin successfully pulled out seeds from cotton bolls.

The cotton gin was a simple invention. Cotton bolls were put into the top of the machine. Then, all one had to do was turn the handle, which turned the cotton through the wire teeth that combed out the seeds. Finally, cotton was pulled away from the wire teeth and out of the cotton gin.

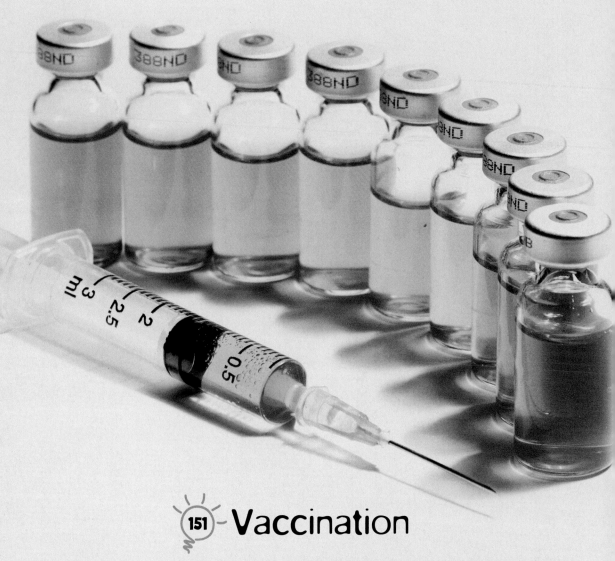

151 Vaccination

In 1796, a dairymaid named Sarah Nelmes consulted Edward Jenner about a rash on her hand. He diagnosed that she had smallpox. Sarah confirmed that one of her cows was recently sick with cowpox.

A few days later, Jenner made a few scratches on a boy's arms and rubbed some material from one of Sarah's pox on them. The boy was suffering from cowpox, but he was well again within a week. This helped Jenner understand that cowpox could pass from person to person and from cow to person.

Edward Jenner conducted a lot of research and studied various cases carefully. His clinical observations and radical case studies explained the viruses better than most scientists. His discovery serves as the basis of modern immunology and his vaccination led to the eradication of smallpox. Even today, smallpox is the only infectious human disease that has been completely eradicated.

152 Battery

A battery produces electricity from a chemical reaction. It is used to power various appliances.

The initial method of generating electricity was by creating a static charge. Otto von Guericke constructed the first electrical machine in 1663. It consisted of a large sulphur globe, which attracted feathers and small pieces of paper when it was rubbed and turned. Guericke proved that the sparks generated were truly electrical.

The first suggested use of static electricity was the so-called "electric pistol", which was invented by Alessandro Volta. An electrical wire was placed in a jar filled with methane gas. When an electrical spark was sent through the wire, the jar exploded. In 1831, Michael Faraday showed how a copper disc provided a constant flow of electricity when it revolved in a strong magnetic field.

In 1836, John F. Daniell, an English chemist, further researched the electro-chemical battery and created an improved cell that produced a steadier current than Volta's device. Until then, all batteries were composed of primary cells, which meant that they could not be recharged.

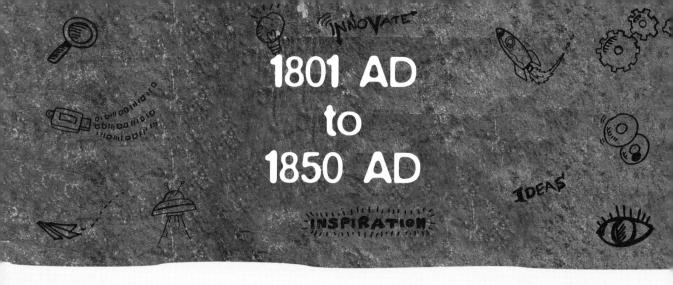

 153 Protractor

Protractors are mathematical drawing instruments that are used to draw and measure angles. They have existed since ancient times, dating back to the 13th century. During that period, European instrument makers created an astronomical observing device called the "torquetum" that also consisted of a semicircular protractor.

A more multifaceted form of the protractor was later designed for plotting the position of a ship on navigational charts. This was invented by US naval captain Joseph Huddart in 1801. This instrument was called a three-arm protractor or station pointer, and was composed of a circular scale that connected to three arms. The centre arm was fixed, whereas the outer two were rotatable, which made them capable of being set at any angle relative to the centre one.

Another similar instrument used by marine navigators is the course protractor. It works as an effective tool that measures the angular distance between magnetic north and the course plotted on a navigational chart.

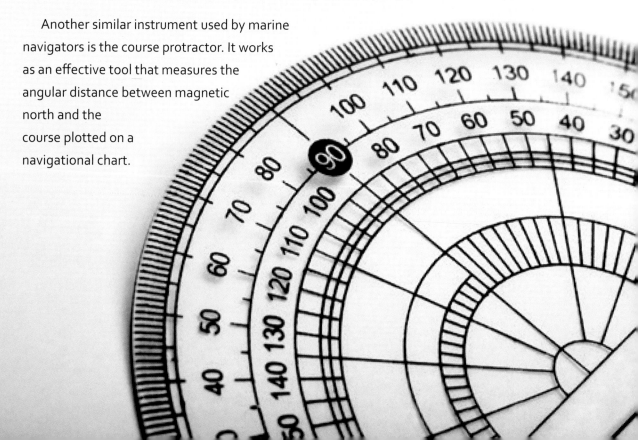

154 Hang Glider

A hang glider is devised to carry a human passenger who is suspended beneath its sail in the air. Hang gliders are usually launched from a high point. They slowly drift down to a lower point.

The modern history of hand gliding begins with the English inventor Sir George Cayley. By 1799, Cayley established a basic design for gliders. In 1804, he flew his first successful model glider. In 1853, Cayley achieved the first successful human glider flight. The next important pioneer was German inventor Otto Lilienthal. In the 1890s, he built around 18 gliders, which he flew himself.

155 Quinine

Quinine is a substance that is found in the bark of the cinchona tree. It was used as a cure for malaria. However, this was later replaced by modern medicine.

In 1817, two French scientists, Pierre-Joseph Pelletier and Joseph Bienaimé Caventou, extracted quinine from the bark of the South American cinchona tree. Before they discovered that quinine cured malaria, the bark of the cinchona tree was first dried, ground to a fine powder and mixed into a liquid before being consumed. This medicine stopped people from shivering in lower temperatures. In 1820, quinine was extracted from the bark of the tree and used as a replacement for the ground bark.

156 Tin Can

It is said that the tin can was invented by the Frenchman Philippe de Girard. He passed the idea to a British merchant named Peter Durand, who revolutionised food preservation when he patented the tin can in 1810. In 1813, John Hall and Bryan Dorkin opened the first commercial canning factory in England. In 1846, Henry Evans invented a machine that manufactured tin cans at a rate of 60 cans per hour. That was a significant increase over the previous rate of only six cans per hour.

Henry Evans invented a method for making a can from a single motion. After a year, Allen Taylor patented his machine-stamped method of producing tin cans.

157 Solar Cells

A solar cell is any device that converts light energy into electrical energy through the process of "photovoltaics". In 1839, French physicist Antoine-César Becquerel developed the technology of solar cells. While experimenting with a solid electrode in an electrolyte solution, he saw a voltage develop when light fell on the electrode. This helped him understand the photovoltaic effect.

The earliest solar cells and panels were not extremely efficient. In 1941, Russell Ohl created the silicon solar cell. In 1954, three American researchers, Gerald Pearson, Calvin Fuller and Daryl Chapin, designed a silicon solar cell capable of six per cent energy conversion under direct sunlight. In 1956, the first solar cells were commercially available.

158 Tractor

The first traction engines were developed during the 1850s. These were widely used for agricultural activities. Prior to these, portable engines powered by steam were used to drive mechanical farm machinery using a flexible belt. The first tractors that were used for ploughing were run by steam engines. Two engines were fixed on opposite sides in a farm to haul a plough back and forth in the space between them using wire cables. Under favourable soil conditions, steam engines were used to haul ploughs directly. Steam-powered engines were used until the 20th century.

The word tractor is derived from the Latin word "trahere", which means to pull. The word "tractor", meaning "an engine meant for wagons or other implements", was coined in the year 1901.

In 1892, in Northeast Iowa, John Froelich invented the first successful gasoline powered engine that could be driven backwards and forwards. During that period, steam-powered engines were used for threshing wheat. John Froelich knew how to operate such equipment, which helped him invent the gasoline-powered engine.

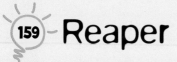

159 Reaper

The reaper is a horse-drawn farm implement that was invented by Cyrus Hall McCormick in 1831. It was created to cut small grain crops. The mechanical reaper replaced the manual cutting of crops, which was done using scythes and sickles. This machine was used to cut down wheat quickly and efficiently.

The reaper harvested wheat and other grains, and could cut around 15 acres a day. Prior to this invention, only three acres could be cut manually. The harvester gained immediate popularity and farmers found the reaper extremely helpful, because it reduced labour costs and the danger of weather destroying crops. The reaper cut the stalks, which fell on a platform. A worker pushed them on the ground with a rake. This task required eight to ten workers.

In 1847, McCormick built a reaper factory in Chicago, next to the Chicago River. In 1848, the McCormick factory manufactured 700 machines. By 1850, this number had doubled. By 1868, 10,000 reapers were made every year. These machines were

160 Stethoscope

Prior to the invention of stethoscope, a physician would listen to a patient's heart by placing his ear over the patient's chest. In 1816, a physician named René Laennec was called to examine a young woman who was believed to have had a heart disease. Based on the medical procedure of the time, Laennec tapped his hand on the patient's back and tried to listen to the resulting sound. However, as the patient was plump, he could not hear anything.

To avoid putting his ear on the young woman's chest, Laennec came up with a simple solution, whereby he rolled a piece of paper into a cylinder and used that to listen to the

also exported to other countries. With each progressing year, the reapers got heavier, stronger and better. The Chicago factory was considered as one of the greatest industrial establishments in USA.

patient's heartbeat. Laennec later created a new instrument from a hollow, wooden cylinder that he called "stethoscope". This word comes from the Greek words "stethos" meaning chest and "skopos" meaning examination.

161 Camera

During the fifth century BC, a Chinese philosopher named Mo Ti observed that a pinhole can form an inverted and focused image when light passes through it and into a dark area. Early cameras were plain boxes that focused light through a pinhole. During the 15th century, good-quality glass lenses were used to focus these images. By the 19th century, chemicals such as silver nitrate allowed a permanent image to be preserved, which established the modern science of photography.

Over time, cameras were developed, rather than being invented by a specific individual. In 1685, Johann Zahn described, but could not build a device that would capture images. In 1825, Nicephore Niepce used bitumen to create the first actual photograph.

The first practical, portable camera was built by Louis Daguerre in 1837. The first practical camera that could be used by a layman was invented by George Eastman in 1888.

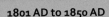

162 Bicycle

The earliest bicycle was a wooden, scooter-like device called a "celerifere". It was invented around 1790 by Comte Mede de Sivrac of France. In 1816, Baron Karl von Drais de Sauerbrun of Germany invented a model with a steering bar attached to the front wheel. He called it a "draisienne". It consisted of two same-sized wheels and the rider sat between the two wheels. The draisienne did not have any pedals. In order to move ahead, one had to propel the bicycle forward using their feet. He exhibited his bicycle in Paris on 6 April, 1818.

Kirkpatrick MacMillan, a blacksmith from Dumfriesshire, Scotland, invented the first bicycle with foot pedals between the 1830s and 1840s. However, he never patented it and his idea did not become popular.

French carriage makers Pierre and Ernest Michaux invented a bicycle in the 1860s, which was an improvement to the previous one. Many early bicycles called "velocipedes", meaning "fast foot", had huge front wheels. It was believed that the bigger the wheel, the faster you could go. Early tyres were wooden and were soon replaced by metal tyres; solid rubber tyres were added much later. A chain with sprockets was added to the bicycle during the 1880s. This was called the "safety bicycle". Air-filled tyres were also added during the 1880s. The gear system that we currently see was added in the 1970s.

163 Suspenders

Suspenders are worn to hold up trousers. The first suspenders date back to 18th century France. Back then, they were strips of ribbons that were attached to the buttonholes of trousers.

During the 1820s, British clothing designer Albert Thurston began to mass manufacture "braces", which is the British word for suspenders. Instead of metal clasps that clasped to the trousers's waistband, these "braces" used leather loops that were attached to buttons on the pants. At the time, British men wore very high-waist trousers and did not use belts.

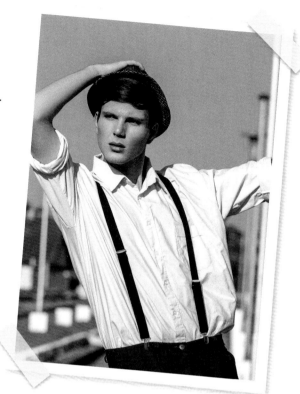

164 Matchstick

A matchstick is a wooden stick that contains a coat of phosphorus mixture at one end. This mixture is ignited by striking the matchstick against the rough surface of the matchbox to produce a flame.

Matchsticks originated around 3500 BC. The Egyptians developed a small, pinewood stick that was coated with a combustible mixture of sulphur. In 1827, the "friction" matchsticks that we use even today were invented by an English chemist named John Walker. The match head had a mixture of antimony sulphide, potassium chlorate, starch and gum.

In 1844, "safety" matches were invented by a Swedish man called Gustaf Erik Pasch and were improved by John Edvard Lundstrom a decade later. These matchsticks ignited only when they were stroked at a specific place.

165 Macintosh Raincoat

In 1823, Scottish chemist Charles Macintosh patented a method for making waterproof garments by using rubber dissolved in coal-tar naphtha for cementing two pieces of cloth together. The now famous Macintosh raincoat is named after Charles Macintosh. This raincoat was first made using the method developed by Charles Macintosh. It led to the creation of the first waterproof fabric. However, the fabric had flaws and was easy to puncture when it was seamed. The natural oil in wool caused the rubber cement to deteriorate. When it was cold, the fabric turned stiff and when it was hot, it turned sticky. With the invention of vulcanised rubber in 1839, Macintosh's fabric improved as it could withstand temperature changes.

166 Bus

Blaise Pascal, a mathematician, inventor, physicist, philosopher, author and general savant, came up with the idea of a bus and secured finance from his friends in the nobility. The system began with seven horse-drawn vehicles running along regular routes. In 1824, John Greenwood established the first modern omnibus service. As the keeper of a toll gate in Pendleton on the Manchester-to-Liverpool turnpike, he purchased a horse and cart with several seats, and began an omnibus service between those two locations. His service did not require prior booking; the driver would pick up or set down passengers anywhere upon their request.

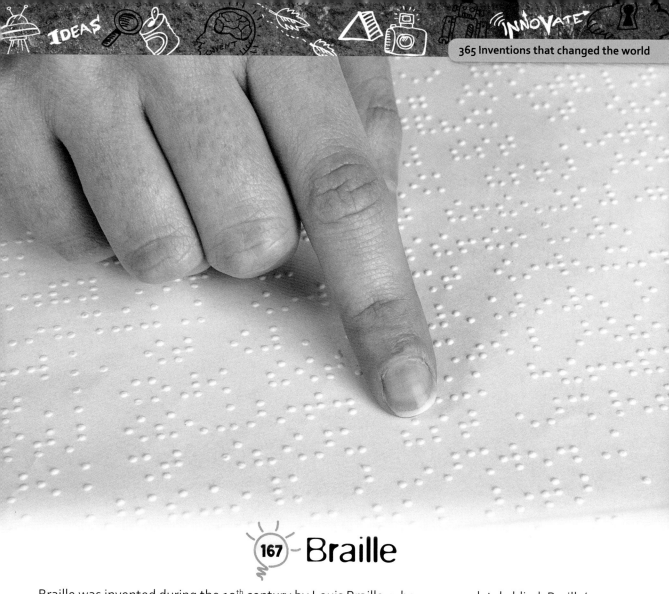

167 Braille

Braille was invented during the 19th century by Louis Braille, who was completely blind. Braille's story goes back to when he was three years old. He injured his eye while he was playing. Though he was offered the best medical attention available at the time, it was not sufficient. An infection soon developed and spread to his other eye, because of which he turned blind in both eyes. It is because of this accident that we have Braille today.

During that time, a system of reading was already in place for the blind; it consisted of tracing a finger along raised letters. However, this system was extremely slow and it was difficult to understand simply by touching the relatively complex letters of the alphabet. Therefore, many people struggled to master the embossed letter system.

Braille is read by passing one's fingertips over characters made from an arrangement of one to six embossed points. The positions of these points represent different alphanumeric characters. Braille can be written with a "Braillewriter" that is similar to a typewriter. A pointed stylus can be used to punch dots through paper using an instrument called a "Braille slate", which has rows of small cells as a guide. Braille has been adapted to almost every known language and is an essential tool for those who are visually challenged.

INSPIRATION

(168) Sewing Machine

In 1790, Thomas Saint, a British inventor, was the first to patent a design for the sewing machine. His machine was to be used only on leather and canvas. However, a working model was not built. In 1814, Austrian tailor Josef Madersperger presented his first sewing machine. The development of this machine had begun in 1807.

In 1830, French tailor Barthélemy Thimonnier had patented a sewing machine that sewed straight seams using a chain stitch. By 1841, Thimonnier had a factory consisting of 80 machines that sewed uniforms for the French Army.

The first sewing machine had all the disparate elements of the previous half-century of innovation. The modern sewing machine was a device built by an English inventor, John Fisher, in 1844 for processing lace materials. His machine was quite similar to the devices that were built by Isaac Merritt Singer and Elias Howe in the following years. However, due to the botched filing of Fisher's patent at the patent office he did not receive due recognition for his contribution towards the modern sewing machine.

169 Handbag

Purses and handbags have their origins in the early pouches that were used to carry seeds, religious items and medicine. With the onset of the railroad, bags were experiencing a revolution. In 1843, there were over 3,000 km of railway lines in Great Britain, because of which many people began travelling by train and women also became more mobile. Professional luggage makers turned the skills of horse travel into those for train travel. Soon, the term "handbag" was coined to describe the new, handheld luggage bags. The famous Hermès bags were founded in 1837 by Thierry Hermès, a harness and saddle maker, while Louis Vuitton was a luggage packer for the Parisian rich.

170 Harvester

The combine harvester is considered to be the modern harvester of wheat. It is called a combine because it "combines" the job of the header and thresher, which were its predecessors. The combine originated in the Midwest, but also had a significant impact on the Northwest and specifically in the state of Washington.

The first combine was made by Hiram Moore in 1836 and was extremely advanced. It was successful because it made farming safer, more profitable and helped food reach many people. However, through the 1800s, the header and the thresher were used individually.

171 - Morse Code

In 1836, Samuel Morse showed how a telegraph system can transmit information over wires. The information was passed as a series of electrical signals. Short signals were referred to as "dits", which were represented as dots. Long signals were referred to as "dahs", which were represented as dashes. With the invention of radio communications, an international version of Morse code came to be used on a large scale.

Morse code depends on specific intervals of time between dits and dahs, between letters and words. The rate of transmitting the Morse code is measured in words per minute. The word "Paris" is used as the standard length of a word. To transmit the word requires 50 units of time. If you transmitted the word five times, you would be transmitting at 5 WPM. An experienced Morse code operator can transmit and receive information at 20-30 WPM.

In 1844, Morse sent his first telegraph message from Washington DC to Baltimore, Maryland; by 1866, a telegraph line had been laid across the Atlantic Ocean from the USA to Europe. Although the telegraph had fallen out of widespread use by the start of the 21st century, and was replaced by the telephone, fax machine and Internet, it had laid the groundwork for the communication revolution that led to all those innovations.

172 Telegraph

In 1794, the non-electric telegraph was invented by Claude Chappe. This system was visual and it used semaphore, a flag-based alphabet. It depended on a line of sight for communication. With time, the optical telegraph was replaced by the electric telegraph. In 1809, a crude telegraph was invented in Bavaria by Samuel Soemmering. He used 35 wires with gold electrodes in water and at the receiving end of 2,000 feet, the message was read by the amount of gas caused by electrolysis. In 1828, the first telegraph in the USA was invented by Harrison Dyar who sent electrical sparks through chemically treated paper tape to burn dots and dashes.

In 1832 Samuel Morse, assisted by Alfred Vail, came up with the idea for an electromechanical telegraph, which he called the "recording telegraph". This commercial application of electricity was made real by their construction of a crude working model in 1835–36. This instrument was probably never used outside Morse's rooms, where it was operated in many demonstrations.

The telegraph was further refined by Morse, Vail and a colleague, Leonard Gale, into a working mechanical form in 1837. The flow of electricity through the wire was interrupted for shorter or longer periods by holding down the key of the device. These dots or dashes were recorded on a printer or could be interpreted orally.

In 1838, Morse perfected his sending and receiving code, as well as founded a corporation, making Vail and Gale his partners.

173 Stamps

In 1680, English merchant William Dockwra and his partner Robert Murray established the London Penny Post, a mail system that delivered letters and small parcels within London for one penny. The postage was prepaid and this payment was confirmed by the use of a hand-stamp that marked the mailed package. The first stamp was black and it was named "Penny Black" It was released on 6 May 1840. Later, several other countries used this idea. To avoid confusion, they put the name of their country on the stamp.

Most other countries have different portraits as stamps, but Great Britain is the only country to use just a picture of the Queen!

The Penny Black had the left profile of Queen Victoria's head, which remained on all British stamps for the following 60 years. Rowland Hill is credited to create the first stamp.

POSTAGE

174 Suspension Bridge

Around 150 years ago, William Hamilton Merritt was the first person to visualise a bridge over the Niagara River. He planned and built the first Well and Canal, making it possible for ships to avoid the Niagara Falls.

In 1846, the governments of Upper Canada and the state of New York consented and started the formation of two companies with the ability to construct a bridge at or near the falls. The companies were called the Niagara Falls Suspension Bridge Company of Canada and the International Bridge Company of New York. Both companies jointly built and owned the bridge. In the autumn of 1847, the bridge companies commissioned Charles Ellet Jr. to construct a bridge at a location selected by the companies along the Niagara River.

The suspension bridge provided an inexpensive solution to the problem of long spans over navigable streams or at other sites where it is otherwise difficult to build piers. British, French, American and other engineers of the late 18th and early 19th centuries faced serious problems of stability and strength against wind forces and heavy loads, failures resulting from storms, heavy snows and droves of cattle.

175 Stapler

The first stapler dates back to 18th century France. The first handmade stapling machines or "fasteners" were developed for King Louis XIV of France during the 1700s. The increase in the use of paper during the 19th century created the need for an efficient paper fastener. Modern paper-fastening devices began with the patent of the first paper fastener on 30th September, 1841, by Samuel Slocum. This basic device stuck pins on paper to hold them together. In 1879, a machine that inserted and clinched a single, pre-formed, metal staple entered the market. It was called "McGill's Patent Single Stroke Staple Press".

176 Aluminium

Aluminium salts were first said to be used by Ancient Greeks and Romans as astringents for dressing their wounds and for fixing dyes. In 1761, Guyton de Morveau suggested that the base alum should be called "alumine". Scientists suspected that an unknown metal existed in alum as early as 1787, but they did not have any method to extract it until 1825. In 1809, Humphry Davy acknowledged the existence of a metal base in alum, which he eventually called aluminium. Hans Christian Oersted, a Danish chemist, was the first to produce tiny amounts of aluminium. After two years, Friedrich Wohler, a German chemist, developed another manner to obtain the metal. By 1845, he produced sufficient samples to determine some of aluminium's basic properties. Wohler's method was improved upon in 1854 by Henri Étienne Sainte-Claire Deville, a French chemist. Deville's process enabled aluminium to be produced commercially.

177 Voltmeter

A voltmeter is defined as an instrument that is used to measure the difference in electrical potential between two points of an electric circuit. The first voltmeter was called a "galvanometer". In 1824, a French physicist and mathematician, Andre-Marie Ampere, invented the first prototype galvanometer. It was the first instrument that could measure the electrical current of a conductor. His invention had its root in the concept of the first galvanometer, as reported by Johann Schweigger on 16 September, 1820. The mechanism of this invention was based on the principle that a magnetic needle would turn away from its position if an electric current was present nearby. The earliest model of the galvanometer or voltmeter consisted of a compass, which was surrounded by a wire coil.

The early galvanometers were not very accurate or consistent. Modern voltmeters measure the potential difference between two points on an electrical circuit. The term "galvanometer" was coined after the surname of an Italian researcher of electricity, Luigi Galvani. In 1791, Galvani discovered that an electric current could cause a frog's leg to jerk.

178 Dirigible

A dirigible or airship is an aircraft that consists of a cigar-shaped gas bag, which is filled with a lighter-than-air gas to provide lift, a propulsion system, a steering mechanism and a gondola that can accommodate passengers, crew and cargo. French inventor Henri Giffard built a steam-powered airship in 1852. However, with the invention of the gasoline engine in 1896, airships were practical to use.

Alberto Santos-Dumont from Brazil was the first to construct and fly a gasoline-powered airship in 1898. During 1910, the "Deutschland" became the first commercial dirigible. Between 1910 and 1914, German dirigibles flew over 1,72,000 km and carried 34,028 passengers and crew without any harm.

179 Safety Pin

The safety pin was invented by a man named Walter Hunt in New York in 1849. It was made from a small piece of metal, which was a combination of copper, iron, aluminium, gold, silver and platinum. These metals were heated and moulded into a small piece.

One afternoon, Walter Hunt had to think of a way to pay a 15-dollar debt. He was sitting at his desk and twisting a piece of wire while trying to think. He twisted the wire for three hours and realised that he had created something different and useful. He called it the safety pin. However, he did not invent the safety pin; he only improved it. It was not the first pin, but it was the first to have a clasp that prevented the sharp edge from poking someone. The first safety pin was invented by the ancient Greeks, Italians and Sicilians.

(180) Fax

Alexander Bain invented the first kind of technology to send an image through a wire. While working on an experimental fax machine between 1843 and 1846, he was able to synchronise the movement of two pendulums through a clock. With that, he managed to scan a message on a line-by-line basis. Frederick Bakewell improved on Bain's invention and created an image telegraph that is very similar to today's fax machine.

Bakewell replaced Bain's pendulums with matching rotating cylinders, which allowed a clearer image through better synchronisation. This telegraph would lift the image from the cylinder with a stylus and place it on the other cylinder through a similar stylus onto chemically-treated paper. Bakewell's image telegraph was successful. It was the first crucial step towards a commercially practical method to send images over a wire.

Following Bain's achievements, a group of inventors made several revisions to the fax machine before arriving at its modern form. Giovanni Caselli created the "pantelegraph", which became the first commercial fax link between Paris and Lyon in France around 1863. Based on Bain's ideas, Caselli's tall, cast-iron machine sent thousands of faxes annually.

(181) Elevator

Evidence suggests that elevators existed in Ancient Rome in 336 BC, built by Archimedes. These were open cars and consisted of a platform with hoists. The first elevator to lift a passenger was designed for French King Louis in 1743.

In 1835, Frost and Stutt developed a counterbalance-type, traction method elevator called the "Teagle". In 1850, a hydraulic elevator working on steam was introduced. This was invented by Elisha G. Otis and called the "safety elevator". Otis solved many obstacles faced by earlier elevators.

The world's first passenger service elevator was installed in a five storey hotel on Broadway, New York, in 1857. Manufactured by the Otis Elevator Company, it was steam-powered, carried a maximum load of 450 kg and had a top speed of 12 m per minute. In 1867, Leon Edoux exhibited the hydraulic-power elevator at the Paris Exposition. With a top speed of 150 m per minute, it grew popular in Europe and the USA.

182 General Anaesthesia

During the 1840s, three new methods of administering unconsciousness came about and were quickly used by doctors to improve their patients' condition. These were nitrous oxide, ether and chloroform. The ability of nitrous oxide to render people unconscious was recognised by English chemist Humphry Davy as early as 1789, who tried it on himself and realised that he didn't feel any pain under its influence. In the 1800s, American chemist Charles Jackson found a stronger anaesthetic – ether. Upon using ether, a person would lose consciousness as well as sensation. On 16 October, 1846, at Massachusetts General Hospital in Boston, the first public demonstration of ether anaesthesia was conducted by William Morton.

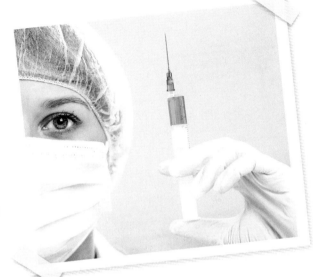

183 Antiseptics

In 1847, Ignaz Semmelweis, a Hungarian obstetrician at the Vienna General Hospital, was trying to find out why one among 30 young mothers was dying of puerperal fever in wards that were looked after by midwives. However, he realised that this number increased to almost one among five mothers in the wards looked after by medical students. Later, he realised that the students were reaching the wards after performing dissections on corpses and treating patients without cleaning and sanitising their hands. This caused infections among the patients. Semmelweis asked the students to wash their hands in diluted bleaching powder before operating. But this led to an increase in the death rate. In 1865, British surgeon Dr Joseph Lister began using carbolic acid to clean his hands and tools. Later, this came to be used as an antiseptic because it did not lead to his patients' deaths.

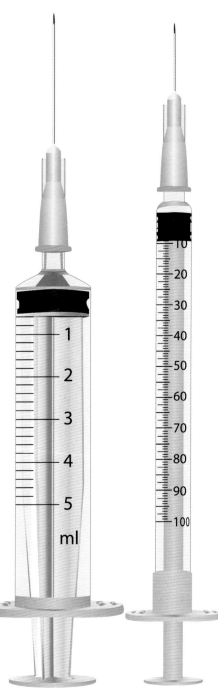

184 Syringe

The first-known device similar to a syringe was used to perform a medical procedure in 900 AD, when Egyptian surgeon Ammar ibn Ali al-Mawsili created a thin, hollow glass tube with suction to remove cataracts from a patient's eyes. During that period, syringes were only used to remove objects or fluid from humans; they were not used to inject.

Hypodermic syringes consist of a hollow needle attached to the syringe. They pierce the skin and inject substances into the bloodstream. Additionally, they are used to extract liquid such as blood from the body.

During the 1850s, French veterinary surgeon Charles Gabriel Pravaz and Scottish doctor Alexander Wood developed a syringe. It consisted of a hollow needle that was sufficiently fine to pierce the skin. Earlier, syringe barrels were made of metal. By 1866, glass was used to make the barrels, but the needles were made from metal. This enabled doctors to check the medication that remained in the barrel.

By the late 1800s, hypodermic syringes were widely available, even though a limited few drugs (less than 2% in 1905) were actually injected. Hypodermic needles were sterilised and reused until the development of disposable syringes. In 1956, a New Zealand pharmacist named Colin Murdoch invented the disposable plastic syringe.

(185) Gyroscope

In 1852, Leon Foucault, a French scientist and physicist, invented the gyroscope. It consists of a wheel or rotor mounted in gimbal rings, which is a set of rings that enable it to turn freely in any direction. If you observe it, you will notice that it is just like a spinning top that has been used as an instrument. A top was first used as an instrument by John Serson in 1743, when he invented the "Whirling speculum".

Foucault used the gyroscope as a tool to study Earth's rotation. A gyroscope is used to maintain or measure the orientation of a particular object. It is also used to construct a gyrocompass, which matches or replaces the magnetic compass used in ships, aircraft, spacecraft and vehicles, to assist in stability or be used as a part of an inertial guidance system.

(186) Bunsen Burner

The Bunsen burner is a common equipment seen in a laboratory. It produces a single open gas flame and is used for heating, sterilising, and combustion of materials. It was invented by Robert Wilhelm Bunsen in 1855. Bunsen was a German chemist and teacher. He invented the Bunsen burner for his research, which required the isolating of chemical substances. The Bunsen burner has a high-intensity, non-luminous flame and does not interfere with the coloured flame that is emitted from the chemicals being tested.

Peter Desaga, a mechanic in the University of Heidelberg, built the first Bunsen burner according to Bunsen's specifications. Bunsen also invented the "hydrojet filter pump", a photometer that measures the intensity of light and the Bunsen battery, which is a chemical battery.

187 Potato Chips

The potato chip was invented in 1853 by George Crum. He was a chef at the Moon Lake Lodge resort in Saratoga Springs, New York, USA. French fries were quite popular at the restaurant where he worked. One day a diner complained that the fries were too thick. Although Crum made a thinner batch, the customer was not satisfied. Crum grew irritated and finally made fries that were too thin to eat with a fork, hoping to annoy the extremely fussy customer. The customer, surprisingly enough, was happy with the food and that's how potato chips were invented!

Crum's chips were originally called Saratoga Chips and potato crunches. They were soon packaged and sold in New England. After a while, Crum opened his own restaurant.

William Tappendon manufactured and marketed the chips in Cleveland, Ohio, in 1895. During the 1920s, salesman Herman Lay sold potato chips to the southern USA. For quite some time, he sold chips from the trunk of his car. In 1926, Laura Scudder, the owner of a potato chip factory in Monterey Park, California, invented a wax-paper, potato chip bag to keep the chips fresh and crunchy, making potato chips even more popular.

188 Synthetic Dyes

The first synthetic or human-made organic dye, mauveine, was discovered by William Henry Perkin while conducting an experiment at his parents' home in 1856. Many synthetic dyes have been prepared since then. These dyes gained popularity and quickly replaced traditional, natural dyes. This is because they cost less, offered a vast range of new colours and imparted better properties to the dyed materials than natural dyes.

Dyes are classified based on how they are used in the dyeing process. Most of the colours that you find today are synthetic dyes. These dyes are used everywhere in everything from clothes to paper and from food to wood.

189 Ohmmeter

An ohmmeter is an electrical instrument that measures electrical resistance, i.e., it opposes any electric current. The Ohmmeter was invented by William Thomson and Lord Kelvin in 1861 to measure very low resistances. The unit of measurement for resistance is ohms (Ω). The original design of an ohmmeter contains a small battery that applies a voltage to a resistance. It uses a galvanometer to measure the electric current through resistance. If the current is known, the drop in voltage across the unknown resistance can be read to give the resistance directly.

INSPIRATION

190 Tuxedo

Also known as a dinner suit or a dinner jacket, the tuxedo is a formal evening suit. During the 1860s, the popularity of outdoor activities among the British middle and upper classes increased. This social boom led to the popularity of the casual lounge suit, which is the standard suit worn in the USA as a countryside alternative to the more formal day wear that was traditionally worn in town. Men also wanted a suit that was similar to the formal evening tailcoat, which was also known as a "dress coat", worn daily in the evenings.

The earliest record of a tailless coat being worn with evening wear is a blue, silk, smoking jacket and matching trousers. This outfit was ordered by the Prince of Wales from Savile Row tailors Henry Poole & Co. It was tailored to be worn at Sandringham, the Prince's informal country estate, and was described as a smoking jacket.

During the 19th century, the accepted formal dress for men was a suit that consisted of long swallowtails. One evening in 1886, young Griswald Lorillard, the heir to a tobacco fortune, shocked the members of his country club by arriving in a dinner jacket without tails.

This revolutionary dinner jacket soon caught on as a fashion statement and the suit took the name of the place where Lorillard introduced it, i.e., the Tuxedo Park, New Jersey. Therefore, this garment came to be called as the "Tuxedo".

Even today, the tuxedo continues to be a popular fashion statement and is worn for formal occasions.

191 Ceiling Fan

Fans date back to the times of Cleopatra. There was a time when people were hired just to move a fan by hand and cool the owner!

The first ceiling fans were seen in the USA around the 1870s. They did not run on electricity; instead they were powered by running water and had two blades instead of four.

Philip Diehl is credited for creating the first ceiling fan out of a fan blade and a sewing machine motor. This was back in 1882. In 1887, he patented his invention. He did not stop there, but continued to add a light fixture followed by a ball joint that was split so that the fan could oscillate. Once that was in place, the idea was further built upon and improvised to perfect the modern day fan; both personal and ceiling fans.

192 Escalator

A machine similar to an escalator first appeared during the mid-19th century, two years after the first passenger elevator was invented. In 1859, Nathan Ames from the state of Michigan, USA, invented something that he called "Revolving Stairs". This invention is acknowledged as the world's first escalator.

The earliest working type of escalator was patented in 1892 by Jesse W. Reno. It was introduced to the public in 1896 as a novelty ride at Coney Island, a theme park in New York.

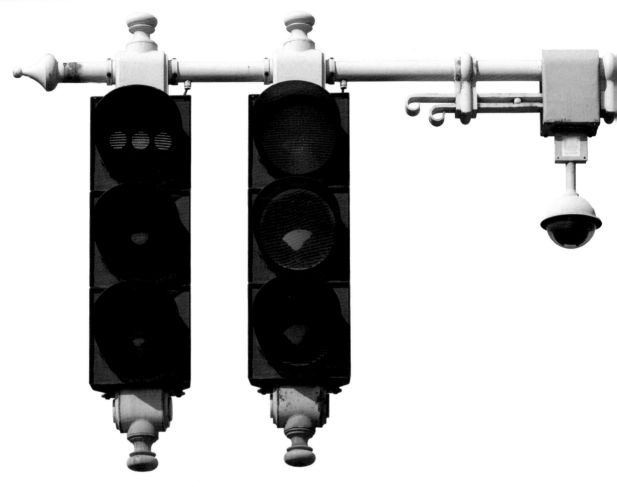

193 Traffic Signal

The first traffic signal was invented in 1868 by J P Knight, a British railway signalling engineer. It was installed outside the Houses of Parliament and was similar to any railway signal of the time. It consisted of waving arms and red-green lamps, which were operated by gas during the nights. Unfortunately it exploded, killing a policeman in the process. The accident did not promote further development until the internal combustion engine was invented.

Modern traffic lights are an American invention. The red-green systems were installed in Cleveland in 1914. Three-colour signals, which were manually operated from a tower in the middle of the street, were first installed in New York in 1918.

The first traffic lights of this kind appeared in 1925 in Britain, on the junction between St. James's Street and Piccadilly. They were manually operated by policemen. Automatic signals were installed in Wolverhampton in 1926. In 1932, the first vehicle-actuated signals in Britain were installed on the junction between Gracechurch Street and Cornhill in the city. Sadly, these were also destroyed by a gas explosion. Standardised red-amber-green signals are now used around the world.

194 Barbed Wire

The earliest wire fences had only one strand of wire, which was constantly broken by the weight of cattle pressing against it. Michael Kelly made a significant improvement to wire fencing. He twisted two wires together to form a cable for barbs, which was known as the "thorny fence". Some inventors wanted to improve upon Michael Kelly's design; Joseph Glidden was one of them.

In 1873 and 1874, patents were issued for various designs to compete against Michael Kelly's invention. Joseph Glidden's design won, because his improvement consisted of simple wire barb locked onto a double-strand wire. Glidden's design made barbed wire more effective; he also invented a method for locking the barbs in place and the machinery to mass produce the wire. Joseph Glidden's US patent was issued on 24 November, 1874.

195 Vacuum Cleaner

Daniel Hess is credited for inventing the first type of vacuum cleaner. It was built in 1860 and was not called a vacuum cleaner; it was called a "carpet sweeper".

Even as early as 1860, the carpet sweeper had a rotating brush that is similar to the vacuum cleaners that we use today. The carpet sweeper had a mechanism on top that contained bellows to create suction. Daniel Hess received a patent in 1860 for his invention. In 1906, motivated by the allergy and asthma attacks that he had experienced upon using his sweeper, janitor James Murray Spangler built an electric vacuum cleaner by using an electric fan motor, soap box, broom handle and a pillowcase. He also added a rotating brush to loosen dirt and debris.

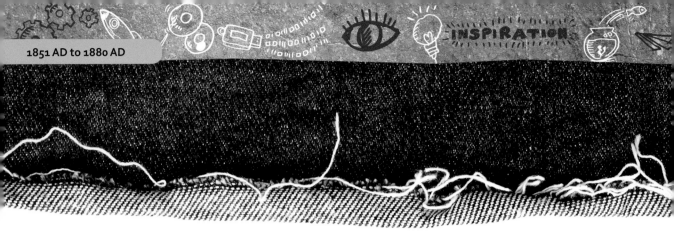

196 Jeans

In 1848, gold was found in California and the well-known Gold Rush began. Gold miners wanted clothes that did not tear easily. In 1853, a clothes supplier, Loeb Strauss, left his home in New York and moved to San Francisco, where he started a wholesale business. Strauss later changed his name from Loeb to Levi.

A big problem with the miners' clothes were the pockets; they tore away easily from the garment. A man called Jacob Davis had the idea of using metal rivets to hold the pockets in place so that they would not tear. Davis wanted to patent his idea, but he did not have sufficient funds. Therefore, in 1872, he wrote to Levi Strauss and proposed the idea to him, asking if he would pay for the patent. Strauss agreed and started making copper-riveted "waist overalls"; that is what jeans were called back then! The patent was granted to Jacob Davis and Levi Strauss & Company on 20th May, 1873. This led to the birth of the blue jeans that we wear even today.

Once their patent was protected, Levi Strauss & Company was the only company making riveted clothing for almost 20 years. When their patent expired, many other manufacturers began to copy their clothing. By then, the public began referring to blue jeans as "Levi's", a name that the company had initially trademarked.

Although jeans were initially invented as work pants, blue jeans became a significant part of popular culture during the 1950s after James Dean wore them in the movie "Rebel Without a Cause". Today, they are worn as casual attire all around the world.

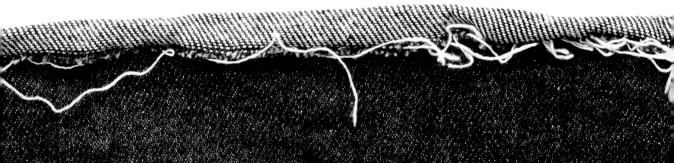

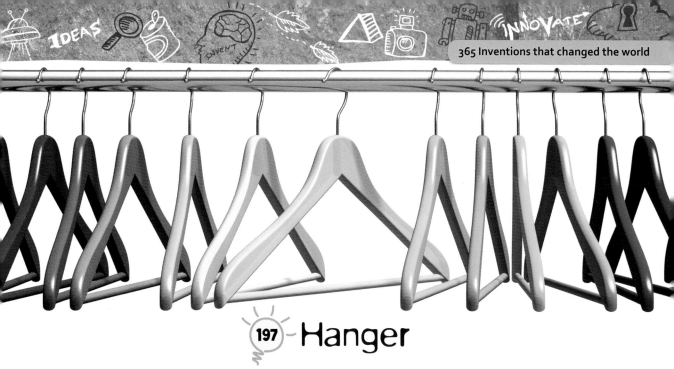

197 Hanger

Some historians thought that the first wooden coat hanger was invented by US president Thomas Jefferson. Most 18th century clothing either hung on hooks or was laid flat in order to store. It was only around 1850 that people started using hangers to hang clothes in wardrobes. The simple wire coat hanger that you know today originated from a clothes hook that was patented in 1869 by O. A. North from New Britain, Connecticut. However, Albert J. Parkhouse, an employee of Timberlake Wire and Novelty Company in Jackson, Michigan, holds the first real wire coat hanger patent.

198 Butter Stick

The butter stick is like a glue stick. It is a Japanese invention, but no information regarding its inventor or date of invention has been recorded. Later, Michael Apeness took the idea from Luke Moon in 1867. Luke Moon invented the butter stick during a game of cricket, when he needed a quick way to butter the scones during his tea break. His team mate, Apeness, decided to use the idea and created his own company. However, the idea did not seem to catch on. Sometimes, the butter could not be applied on the bread and would end up tearing the bread. People found it easier to apply butter with a butter knife instead of using the butter stick.

199 Paper Clip

The first paper clip was patented in 1867 by Samuel B. Fay. This clip was originally made for the purpose of attaching tickets to cloth, although the patent recognised that it could also be used to attach papers together. There were no advertisements or any other mention of the Fay design until 1896.

In 1896, Fay announced that D. S. Gorman was the New York distributor for a new paperclip named "Clinch". It used the Fay design. Additionally, in 1896, the Cinch Clip Co. in Buffalo, New York, was identified as the manufacturer of a paper clip named Cinch, which also used the Fay design. Therefore, it is unlikely that paper clips with the Fay design had any sales, let alone impressive ones, before 1896.

However, during the late 1890s and for decades afterwards, the Fay design was widely advertised under many brand names and effectively used for fastening papers. In 1918, the brand name "Fay" was used by the American Clip Company for a paper clip with the Fay patent design. A second type of a paper clip design was patented by Erlman J. Wright in 1877. This clip was advertised to be used for newspapers during that time.

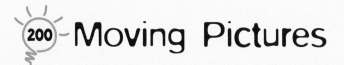

200 Moving Pictures

The first machine patented in the USA that showed animated pictures or movies was a device called the "wheel of life" or "zoopraxiscope". It was patented in 1867 by William Lincoln; moving drawings or photographs were watched through a slit in the zoopraxiscope. This significantly differed from what is used today. Modern motion picture making started with the invention of the motion picture camera. Frenchman Louis Lumiere is often credited for inventing the first motion picture camera in 1895. Many others had made similar inventions around the same time as Lumiere. Eadweard Muybridge conducted motion-sequence, still photograph experiments, and is called the "Father of Motion Pictures" even though he did not make films like the ones that exist today.

201 Dynamite

Alfred Nobel found the detonator or blasting cap for detonating nitro-glycerine in 1863. This detonator used a strong shock rather than heat combustion to ignite the explosives. The Nobel Company was the first to produce nitro-glycerine and dynamite.

Italian chemist Ascanio Sobrero invented nitro-glycerine in 1846. Alfred Nobel realised that nitro-glycerine is extremely volatile in nature and mixed it with silica, causing the paste to turn malleable. He filled cylindrical containers with this mixture and ignited them, which caused a blast. He further improved his dynamite by inserting a blasting cap that could be ignited with a fuse. In 1867, Nobel received a patent number for his dynamite.

202 Typewriter

The invention of the typewriter is credited to a Wisconsin newspaperman, Christopher Latham Sholes. When his printers did not work, he made a few unsuccessful attempts to invent a typesetting machine. He then collaborated with another printer, Samuel Soule and invented a numbering machine. A friend, Carlos Glidden, suggested that they should invent a machine that prints letters.

The three of them tried to invent such a machine. They did not know much and made several mistakes. After a lot of hard work, the invention finally took form and the inventors were granted patents in June and July 1868. Investor James Densmore bought a share in the machine, buying out Soule and Glidden. Densmore furnished the funds to build about 30 models in succession, each a little better than the previous one. The improved machine was patented in 1871.

203 Cable Car

On 17 January, 1871, Andrew Smith Hallidie from San Francisco patented the first cable car. This led to a decrease in the number of horses doing the work of moving people around on steep roadways.

The cable car was introduced in San Francisco on Sacramento and Clay in 1873. The cars were pulled by an endless cable running in a slot between the rails and passing over a steam-driven shaft in the powerhouse. The system was well-adapted to operate on steep hills and was extensively used in San Francisco and Seattle.

204 Planned Language

The first "planned language" is said to be developed by a Polish ophthalmologist, Lazarus Zamenhof, who felt that there would be less confusion if people spoke a common language. While developing his language, Zamenhof did not use popular European languages such as English, French, German and Russian, because he did not wish to give these speakers an upper hand. He developed his language on the Romance languages that used the 28-letter alphabet, few words, six verbs ending without irregularities and an easy set of grammar rules. He formulated a language called "Lingvo Internacia". It is believed that this language is easier than Spanish.

In 1878, Zamenhof turned 19. By then, he had developed a bridge between cultures. Nine years later, his first book of instruction was published under the pseudonym "Esperanto", meaning "person is hoping" in Lingvo Internacia. At present, around two million people around the world can speak Esperanto, as it has become famous.

Several other languages have been invented, which include Basic English, Glosa and Eurolang. However, only two languages, in addition to Esperanto, have been successful.

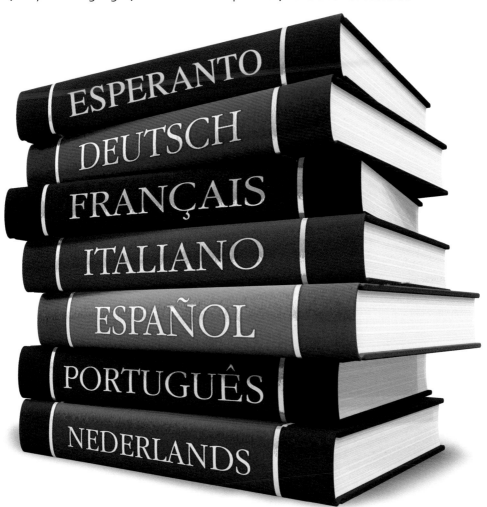

205 - Electrometer

An electrometer measures an electrical potential, i.e., volts or charge. A charge and an electric potential are directly related. By measuring the change that is accumulated over time, the current can also be determined. The basic quadrant electrometer was developed by Lord Kelvin in the 1860s. The earliest versions were kept inside a "bird cage" or box. The bird cage electrometers were named after the Faraday cage that was used to protect the instrument from stray electrostatic charges. In some cases, air currents were protected by a glass bell jar, which could affect their operation. The other common approach was to house the electrometer inside a wooden box with a glass front.

206 - Mauve

In 1856, 18-year-old William Perkin was carrying out experiments to make quinine, a cure for malaria. While doing this, Perkin accidentally made a bright, purple substance that permanently dyed silk. He patented the process and convinced his father to invest the family savings in a dye factory at Greenford, West London. Some French chemists had also made a mauve dye during the same time, but they used a different process. As luck would have it, Empress Eugenie, wife of Emperor Napoleon III of France, decided that mauve matched the colour of her eyes. She had dresses made in mauve silk. She was considered a fashion icon during that time. Within five years, Perkin had earned a fortune, as mauve became the most fashionable colour in Victorian Britain. The discovery led to a revolution in the dyeing industry.

207 Telephone

Antonio Meucci, an Italian immigrant, began to create a design for a talking telegraph or telephone in 1849. In 1871, he filed an announcement for the invention or "caveat" of his design of a talking telegraph. Due to many problems, Meucci could not renew his caveat. His role in the invention of the telephone was overlooked until the US House of Representatives passed a resolution on 11 June, 2002, honouring Meucci's contributions and work. In 1860, 16 years before Bell claimed that he invented the telephone, Meucci demonstrated his "teletrofono" in New York. However, he could not afford the $250 required to register a patent. In the 1870s, Alexander Graham Bell patented his telephone. He built his invention while working at a school for the deaf.

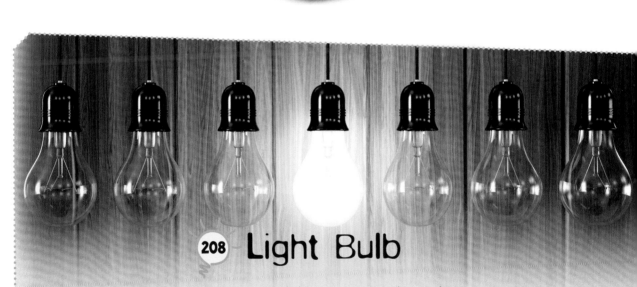

208 Light Bulb

The first electric light was made by an English scientist named Humphry Davy in 1800. He connected wires to a battery and a piece of carbon. This made the carbon glow, which produced light. Around 1860, English physicist Sir Joseph Wilson Swan wanted to create a practical, long-lasting electric light. He found that a carbon paper filament did the job, but burnt quickly.

Thomas Alva Edison experimented with thousands of different filaments. In 1880, Edison discovered the right filament, which helped him invent the light bulb.

209 Altimeter

French physicist Louis Paul Cailletet invented the altimeter in 1877-78. The altimeter is an instrument that measures vertical distance at a reference level. In 1928, German inventor Paul Kollsman invented an accurate barometric altimeter which was named the "Kollsman Window". It was used to check and verify a particular location. It is used in aeroplanes for the pilot to know how high they are flying above the sea level. An altimeter is also used as an altitude measuring device for an object at some fixed level.

210 Vending Machine

During the early 1880s, the first coin operated vending machines were introduced in London, England. They gave out post cards. Around the same time, English publisher and bookshop owner Richard Carlisle invented a vending machine for selling books. In 1888, the Thomas Adams Gum Company started the first vending machines in the USA. These machines were installed on subway platforms in New York City and sold tutti-frutti gum. In 1897, the Pulver Manufacturing Company added animated figures to its gum machines as an added attraction. In 1907, the round, candy-coated gumball was introduced, followed by gumball vending machines.

211 Pasteurisation

Pasteurisation is a process that kills harmful bacteria growing in dairy products, especially in the absence of refrigeration. This process was invented by Louis Pasteur in 1864. During that time, the discovery was a revolutionary one. It enabled milk to be consumed over a period of time and prevented many illnesses. Centuries before pasteurisation was discovered, cheesemaking originated in order to preserve milk products in the absence of refrigeration.

Pasteur was trained in science and working at the Lille University in France, when a few winemakers invited him to solve a problem they were facing. They could not understand why certain wines were turning bad rather quickly as compared to the others.

Using a microscope, Pasteur discovered that the yeast used to make wine and beer contains different bacteria. Some of the bacteria helps in producing alcohol from sugar, while other bacteria render the drink bad after it has been made. Pasteur's simple solution was to heat the wine for a short time to kill the harmful bacteria so that the drink would not spoil quickly. This idea, which came to be known as pasteurisation, was hugely successful and was adopted to help preserve a wide range of other foods and drinks.

212 Phonograph

While working towards improving the telegraph and the telephone, famous inventor Thomas Edison found a solution to record sound on tinfoil coated cylinders. He created a machine that consisted of two needles: one was used for recording and the other was used for playback. When Edison spoke into the mouthpiece, the sound got indented onto the cylinder by the recording needle.

In 1877, Thomas Alva Edison created his first phonograph. It worked by translating air vibrations that were created by a human voice into minute indentations on a sheet of tinfoil. This sheet was placed over a metallic cylinder. Then, the machine reproduced the sounds that caused the indentations.

213 Microphone

The word "microphone" was coined in 1827 by Sir Charles Wheatstone. However, it was not invented until 1876. Emile Berliner is the inventor of the microphone. He was particularly interested in improving Alexander Graham Bell's invention of the telephone. He studied and experimented on several methods to record, reproduce and repeat sounds. His observations led to an innovation.

The invention of the microphone was not a part of an individual device by itself. Emile Berliner invented the microphone in 1876 for the telephone, so that the sound in telephones became more audible.

214 Colour Photography

In 1861, Thomas Sutton collaborated with theoretical physicist James Clerk Maxwell to take three separate exposures of a tartan ribbon through red, green and blue filters. The developed negatives were launched through separate magic lanterns on to a screen using the same coloured filters. This created a single image, giving birth to the principle of colour photography at the Royal Institution in London. The first permanent colour photograph was taken in 1861 by Maxwell.

215 Milking Machine

It is believed that milking machines were used around 300 BC by the ancient Egyptians. They used hollow wheat stems that were inserted in a cow's teats to milk it. Hand-milking was popular in USA till about the 1860s, when American inventors began finding more efficient ways to milk cows. In 1860, Lee Colvin invented the first hand-held pump device.

In 1879, Anna Baldwin patented a milking machine. It used a large rubber cup that connected the cow's udder to a pump lever and bucket. Working the pump lever pulled the milk out of the udder and into the bucket. Baldwin's invention was one of the earliest American patents.

(216) Metal Detector

In 1881, Alexander Graham Bell invented the first metal detector. When President James Garfield was shot by an assassin's bullet, Bell hastily invented a simple metal detector in an unsuccessful attempt to locate the fatal slug. Bell's metal detector was an electromagnetic device that he called the "induction balance". The first metal detector that Bell used on President Garfield was made using a large primary coil with a smaller secondary coil fixed to it. The coils were mounted on a handle for scanning.

In 1925, Gerhard Fischer invented a portable metal detector. In 1931, his model was first sold commercially. Fischer is responsible for the first large-scale production of metal detectors.

Metal detectors work in different ways. The science behind one of the simpler kind of metal detectors is that it contains a coil of wire, which is wrapped around the circular head at the end of the handle. This is known as the transmitter coil.

When electricity flows through the transmitter coil, a magnetic field is created all around it. As one sweeps the detector over the ground, the magnetic field moves around too. If the detector moves over a metallic object, the moving magnetic field affects the atoms inside the metal, which helps one detect the presence of the metallic object. Metal detectors are now commonly used at airports and other public places.

217 Egg Beater

An egg beater, also known as a mixer, is a kitchen appliance that is used for stirring, whisking or beating eggs and other ingredients.
On 5th February, 1884, Willis Johnson of Cincinnati, Ohio, patented an improved mechanical egg beater.

Willis Johnson had invented an early mixing machine, not just an egg beater. His device was not intended for beating eggs only. He had designed his mixer to beat eggs and also to mix batter and other baking ingredients. It was a double-acting machine consisting of two chambers. This invention could allow batter to be beaten in one section and eggs in the other, or one section could be cleaned while the other section could continue to mix the batter.

218 Rabies Vaccine

Louis Pasteur first studied the saliva of animals and humans who died of rabies and confirmed the presence of a specific microbe that was too small to be seen through a microscope. He then examined tissue from the brain and spinal cord of some of the victims and found that the virus was present in them. Pasteur was sure that he could make a vaccine using weakened strains of the disease-causing organism or virus.

Pasteur was confident that he could prevent the dreaded disease in dogs, but he did not test the drug on humans. However, on 6th July, 1885, the decision to perform a human trial was made for him. A nine-year-old boy, Joseph Meister, was brought to him by his distraught mother. Joseph had been bitten many times by a rabid dog in his village. Pasteur administered the vaccine and within weeks, the boy was cured.

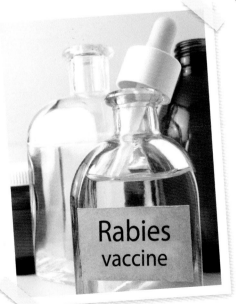

Rabies vaccine

INSPIRATION

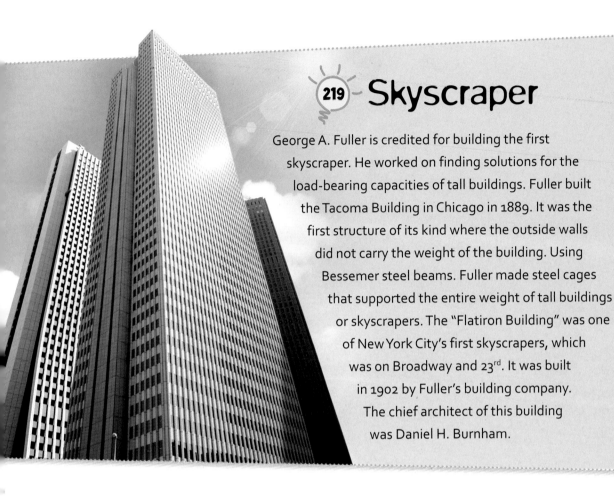

219 Skyscraper

George A. Fuller is credited for building the first skyscraper. He worked on finding solutions for the load-bearing capacities of tall buildings. Fuller built the Tacoma Building in Chicago in 1889. It was the first structure of its kind where the outside walls did not carry the weight of the building. Using Bessemer steel beams. Fuller made steel cages that supported the entire weight of tall buildings or skyscrapers. The "Flatiron Building" was one of New York City's first skyscrapers, which was on Broadway and 23rd. It was built in 1902 by Fuller's building company. The chief architect of this building was Daniel H. Burnham.

220 Punching Cards

The basic punched card was originally invented by Herman Hollerith. It was first used for the tabulation of important statistics by the New York City Board of Health and many other states. After using this system on a trial basis, punched cards were used in the 1890 census.

Hollerith's idea of using punched cards for data processing came after he saw punched cards being used to control Jacquard looms. Jacquard, who was working in France around 1810, came up with the idea of using holes punched in cardstock in order to control the pattern that a loom weaves.

221 Catheter

Catheters have been used since ancient times. Back then, Syrians made catheters out of reeds. The Greeks used hollow, metal tubes that were inserted through the urethra into the bladder to let out the liquid. In modern medicine, the use of a catheter was first introduced by Dr N. B. Sornborger, who patented the syringe and catheter in 1868. Mechanically, it is a weak polymer that is prone to breakage, which can lead to complications such as a part of the catheter remaining in the body even after being removed.

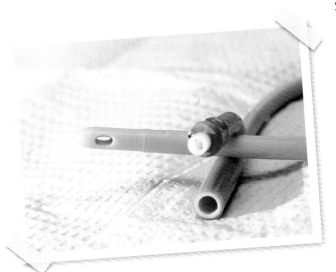

It was during the early 1900s that a man from Dublin named Walsh, along with Scottish urologist Norman Gibbon, created the standard catheter that is used in hospitals today. We know it as "the Gibbon-Walsh catheter".

222 Gramophone

Emile Berliner, a German immigrant working in Washington DC, patented a system that successfully recorded sound on 8 November, 1887. Berliner was the first to stop recording on cylinders and start recording on flat discs or records instead.

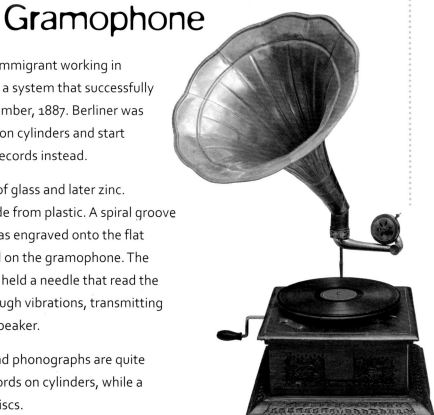

The first records were of glass and later zinc. Eventually, they were made from plastic. A spiral groove with sound information was engraved onto the flat record. The record rotated on the gramophone. The "arm" of the gramophone held a needle that read the grooves in the record through vibrations, transmitting the information into the speaker.

While gramophones and phonographs are quite similar, a phonograph records on cylinders, while a gramophone records on discs.

INSPIRATION

223 - Car

Gottlieb Daimler is credited for inventing what is often referred to as the prototype of the modern gas engine. This engine consisted of a vertical cylinder, where fuel was injected through a carburettor. This invention was patented in 1885.

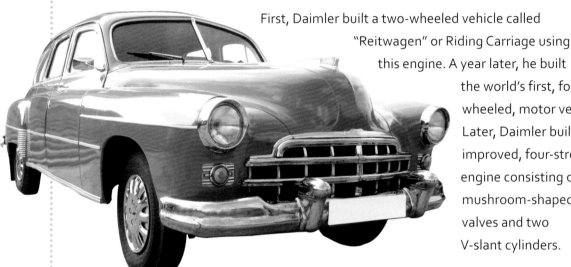

First, Daimler built a two-wheeled vehicle called "Reitwagen" or Riding Carriage using this engine. A year later, he built the world's first, four-wheeled, motor vehicle. Later, Daimler built an improved, four-stroke engine consisting of mushroom-shaped valves and two V-slant cylinders.

224 - Light Meter

A light meter is a device that is used to measure the amount of light in a specific context. In photography, it is used to determine the proper exposure for a photograph. A light meter includes a computer that could be either digital or analogue. This allows the photographer to determine which shutter speed and f-number should be selected for an optimum exposure, given a certain lighting situation and film speed.

The earliest types of light meters were called "extinction meters". Alfred Watkins is credited with inventing the "Bee Meter", which was patented in April 1890. This was the first light meter to measure the relative intensity of light. It helped assign a numerical value to light.

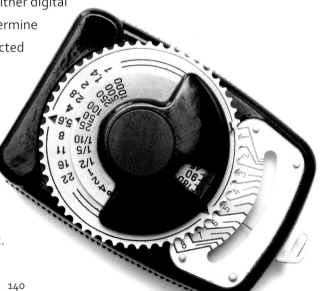

(225) Watt Metre

A watt metre is an instrument that measures electrical energy in watt hours, which essentially accumulates or averages readings. In 1872, Samuel Gardiner first patented an electric metre. This was a DC lamp-hour metre. It was a clock with an electromagnet that started and stopped the mechanism.

The first specimen of the AC kilowatt-hour metre was produced on the basis of Hungarian Ottó Bláthy's patent and was named after him. It was presented by the Ganz Works at the Frankfurt Fair during the autumn of 1889. The first induction kilowatt-hour metre was also marketed by the same factory at the end of the same year. These were the first alternating-current, watt-hour metres. They were known as Bláthy-metres.

The AC kilowatt hour metres that we use at present operate on the same principle as Bláthy's original invention.

Watt metres measure and record the electric power that flows through a circuit over a period of time. There are several different types of watt-hour metres. Each of them consists of a small electric motor and a counter. A specific amount of current flowing through the circuit is diverted in order to run the motor. The speed at which the motor turns is the same as the current in the circuit. Therefore, each revolution of the motor's rotor corresponds to a given amount of current flowing through the circuit.

226 Electric Chair

In 1881, a dentist named Alfred P. Southwick watched an intoxicated man accidentally shock himself to death. This led him to create a new method to execute people who were on death row. He felt that it would be a good alternative to hanging, because it would be quick and painless. Employees from Thomas Edison's company designed the first electric chair. They used a generator from the rival Westinghouse Corporation to power the chair, so customers would think that Westinghouse's products were deadly. They even tried to popularise "Westinghouse" as a word to describe the chair, but the word "electrocute" became more popular. It was in 1888 that New York decided to replace hanging with death by electricity. That is when the electric chair came to be used.

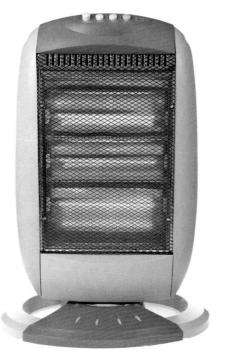

227 Electric Heater

Thomas Edison is considered to be the inventor of the electric heater, as electricity and the light bulb produce heat as well as light. The basic electric heater has undergone minimal change and is still used in the same manner. The electric heater converts energy into heat. Electric current flows through the metal component, which radiates heat throughout the room.

In 1905, Albert Marsh discovered chromel, which is made of four parts nickel and one part chromium. This was the first metallic combination to serve as a heating element. During that time, this new alloy was 300 times stronger than other heating elements available in the market. Therefore, Marsh was dubbed as the father of the electrical heating industry. A patent for the development of chromel was acquired in 1906.

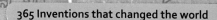

228 Jukebox

Music boxes and player pianos were the first forms of automated, coin-operated, musical devices. These instruments used paper rolls, metal discs or metal cylinders to play a song on the instrument, or instruments, that were enclosed within the device. In the 1890s, these devices were joined by machines that used actual recordings instead of physical instruments. In 1918, Hobart C. Niblack patented an apparatus that automatically changed records, leading to the first selective jukebox of its kind being introduced in 1927 by the Automated Musical Instrument Company.

229 Crescent Wrench

The crescent wrench, also referred to as a spanner, is an important tool that has been in use for almost two centuries. Its mechanism is very simple. The crescent wrench works as a lever; it has notches that help with the grip. The torque is created by pulling the wrench along right angles to either loosen or tighten something. The first patent for a wrench was granted to Solymon Merrick in 1835.

The adjustable wrench, which was once known as the "English Key", was first invented by English engineer Richard Clyburn in 1842. Edwin Beard Budding, another English engineer, is also credited with the invention of the wrench. Many improvements were made on the original model. In 1885, Enoch Harris created and patented a spanner whose jaw width and handle angles could be adjusted.

INSPIRATION

230 Radio

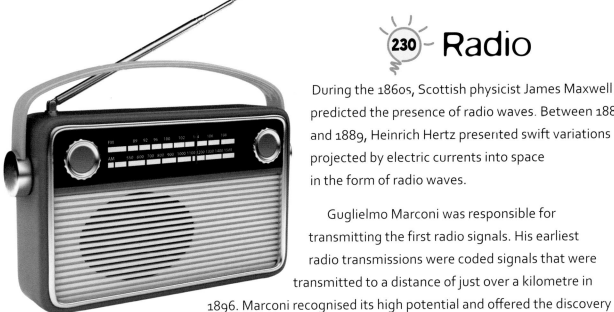

During the 1860s, Scottish physicist James Maxwell predicted the presence of radio waves. Between 1885 and 1889, Heinrich Hertz presented swift variations projected by electric currents into space in the form of radio waves.

Guglielmo Marconi was responsible for transmitting the first radio signals. His earliest radio transmissions were coded signals that were transmitted to a distance of just over a kilometre in 1896. Marconi recognised its high potential and offered the discovery to the Italian Government, but they rejected it. He patented it and continued his experiments after moving to England. In 1898, he flashed the results of Kingstown Regatta to Dublin Newspaper's office, making it the first public broadcast of a sports event. In the following year, he opened his radio factory in Essex, thus creating links between France and Britain. In 1901, he established a link with the USA. Marconi shared the Nobel Prize in Physics with Karl Braun for their contributions towards the wireless telegraph in 1909.

231 Toaster

A British company called Crompton and Company invented the first electric toaster in 1893. During that time, the company also made space heaters. Rookes Crompton's design had iron heating coils that were completely exposed. Users had to flip the bread by hand to brown the bread on both sides. From a safety perspective, the Crompton design would never work today, but it was very easy to clean. General Electronics (GE) created the first commercially successful toaster, which it patented in 1909. Frank Shailor invented this toaster and GE claims credit for its invention, although two other toasters were available in the market during the same time.

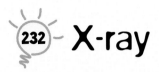
232 X-ray

In 1895, Wilhelm Conrad Röntgen accidentally discovered the X-ray. He was experimenting with his cathode ray generator, when he noticed that beams sent out from the machine were able to penetrate and reach deeper layers than he thought possible. Once he understood the machine's capability, he improved the technique so he could demonstrate it to the public.

As an experiment, Röntgen X-rayed his wife's hand and found that the machine captured a picture of her bones beneath the skin. This amazed Röntgen and he set out to make the scientific community aware of his findings. Röntgen named his discovery "X-radiation" because of the rays that the machine used to see through deep layers of the body. His discovery transformed medicine overnight. Within a year, the first radiology department was opened in a Glasgow hospital. The departmental head produced the first pictures of a kidney stone and a penny lodged in a child's throat.

Röntgen is considered to be the father of the X-ray machine. However, a major improvement to the X-ray process came in 1903 because of another inventor, W.D. Coolidge. He developed the X-ray tube, which is one of the main reasons why X-rays are so effective even today.

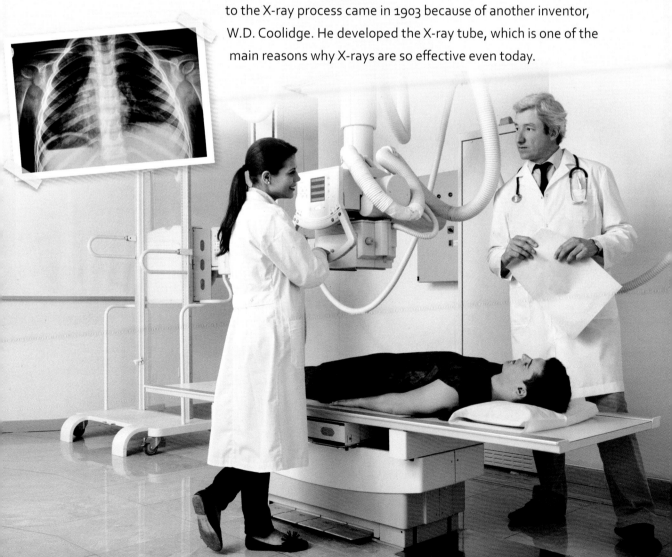

233 Motion Camera

Most of us are grateful for the invention of the motion camera, a device that records all the movies and television shows that we love to watch. Thomas Edison is often credited with inventing the first motion picture camera in 1891 using a kinetoscope. His ideas are a culmination of several theories and advances towards the construction of a camera-like device that captured motion.

The original version of this machine was the magic lantern, an early version of a slide projector. It enabled images to pass through a lens using light, which was often supplied by a kerosene lamp. However, it took a long time before these crude projection machines were improved in order to be able to simulate motion. Two centuries after the invention of the magic lantern, Simon Ritter von Stampfer of Vienna created the Stroboscope in 1832, where drawings from the rim of a disc were viewed through the slits in a second disc which simulated motion. Various versions of these ideas emerged during the 1830s.

Scottish inventor William Dickson began experimenting with Eastman's Celluloid film and soon realised that motion pictures depend on light passing through a frame. He would cut film sheets into strips and perforate the edges, an idea also approached by Praxinoscope inventor Reynaud. Dickson used a stop-motion device that took pictures onto strips of emulsion-covered celluloid. From the negatives, Dickson made a positive print, placing it in a box-shaped structure that was propelled by a battery operated motor. He ran the strips on a loop between an electric lamp and shutter.

This was the creation of what is considered to be the first motion picture film. Dickson's experiments were the first actual motion pictures to be recorded.

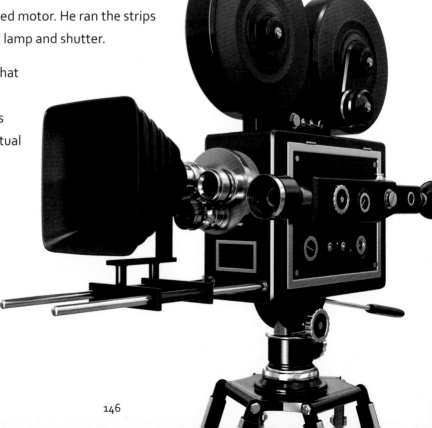

234 Torch/Flashlight

Towards the end of the 19th century, the invention of the dry cell battery made portable lighting possible. Conrad Hubert, a Russian immigrant living in New York, founded "The American Electrical Novelty and Manufacturing Company". This company marketed and sold battery-powered inventions.

Hubert was an inventor himself, but it was his British employee, David Misell, who invented the first flashlight in 1898. He received a patent for his invention in the following year. The device was branded as the "Eveready Flash Light". Later, Hubert renamed his company as "Eveready".

235 Cornflakes

In 1898, during an attempt to make granola, W. K. Kellogg and his brother, Dr John Harvey Kellogg, made what we fondly know and consume as cornflakes today. The concept of breakfast changed forever when they accidentally flaked wheat berry.

W. K. Kellogg kept experimenting until he also flaked corn and created a delicious recipe for the famous Kellogg's Cornflakes. In 1906, W. K. Kellogg opened the "Battle Creek Toasted Cornflake Company" and hired his first 44 employees after careful scrutiny. Together, they created the initial batch of Kellogg's® Cornflakes®.

236 - Cotton Candy

Cotton candy is made from finely-granulated sugar that is heated and spun into slim threads. It was invented in 1897 by William Morrison and John C. Wharton, candymakers from Nashville, Tennessee, USA. They invented a device that heated sugar in a spinning bowl containing tiny holes. This process formed a treat that they originally called "Fairy Floss". As the bowl spun around, caramelised sugar was forced through the tiny holes, making feathery candy that melted in the mouth.

Morrison and Wharton introduced cotton candy to the world at the St. Louis World's Fair in 1904. They sold huge amounts of cotton candy for 25 cents a box. They sold about 68,655 boxes at that fair. The term "cotton candy" began to grow popular around 1920 in USA. In the United Kingdom, this treat is called candyfloss.

237 - Remote Control

In June 1956, the practical television remote controller was introduced in the USA. However, research shows that in 1893, a remote control for television was described by Nikola Tesla in a US patent. The Germans used remote-controlled motorboats during World War I. The late 1940s saw the first non-military uses of remote controls; for instance, automatic garage door openers.

Zenith engineer Eugene Polley created the first wireless TV remote, the "Flash-matic", in 1955. It operated using four photocells placed in the four corners of a TV screen. The viewer had to use a directional flashlight to activate the functions. However, the Flash-matic turned out to be problematic on sunny days, when the sunlight sometimes randomly changed channels!

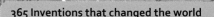

238 Aspirin

On 10 October, 1897, Aspirin was developed in Germany by a chemical process by research chemist Felix Hoffman. He was looking for something to relieve the pain caused by arthritis to his father. He studied French chemist Charles Gergardt's experiments and rediscovered acetylsalicylic acid or aspirin, as it is known today.

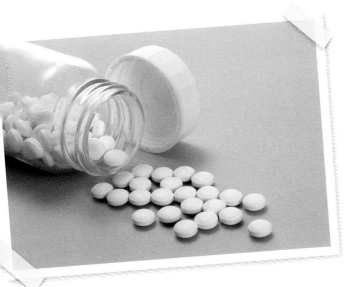

Even today, aspirin continues to be known as the most versatile and effective medicine on a pharmacist's shelf. As doctors are now increasingly recognising its properties, they have acknowledged that the drug does not just relieve aches and pains, but is also instrumental in preventing many serious, life-threatening conditions.

239 Speedometer

A speedometer is a device that is placed in a vehicle to measure and display the speed of that vehicle. It is essential for safety on roads and highways around the world. It was invented in 1888 by a Croatian scientist named Josip Belusic. It was first called a "velocimeter". The speedometer can be seen on various other forms of transportation as well. The digital speedometer on an aeroplane is called an "airspeed indicator", whereas the one on a boat is referred to as the "pit log". Speedometers have an error tolerance of about 10% as the car and the device can wear out over time.

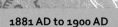

240 Zeppelin

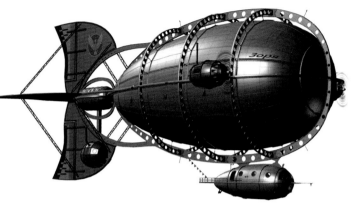

In 1900, a German military officer named Ferdinand Zeppelin invented a rigid-framed airship that came to be known as the "Zeppelin". Ferdinand Zeppelin flew the world's first untethered rigid airship, the LZ-1, on 2nd July, 1900, near Lake Constance, Germany. It carried five passengers.

The cloth-covered zeppelin or dirigible, which was the prototype for many subsequent models, had an aluminium structure, 17 hydrogen cells and two 15-horsepower Daimler internal combustion engines. Each of these engines were turning two propellers. The first zeppelin was 420 feet long and 38 feet wide. During its first flight, it flew about 6 km in 17 minutes and reached a height of 1,300 feet.

241 Tank

The enormously armoured vehicle that we know as a "tank" was first used during World War I. By the beginning of World War II, the tank had been improved upon and served as a technological weapon for soldiers. In 1903, a French Captain, Levavasseur, proposed a project to create a tank that would work just like a caterpillar. It would self-propel and provide 100% armour protection. This was supposed to be known as the Levavasseur Design Project. However, this idea was done away with in 1908, as they discovered that a similar product had already been invented by engineer David Roberts. Günther Burstyn and engineer Lancelot Mole were the creators of newly designed models of the tank. However, they were rejected by the government administrations at the time.

(242) Dry Cell Battery

During the 1880s, German scientist Carl Gassner invented the first dry cell. He used zinc for the outer casing that housed the cell's other components. He also used the sealed zinc container as the anode. The cathode was surrounded by a carbon rod. Gassner also added zinc chloride to the electrolyte. This reduced the corrosion of zinc when the cell was idle, which led it to have a very good shelf life. A common dry cell battery is the zinc-carbon battery, which uses a cell that is also called the "Leclanché cell".

(243) Motorbike

Gottlieb Daimler invented the first motorcycle in 1885, with one wheel in the front and one at the back. It had a smaller spring-loaded outrigger wheel on each side. He built this motorbike by teaming up with Karl Benz to form the Daimler-Benz Corporation.

These motorbikes were mainly constructed from wood. The wheels were made of the iron-banded wooden spokes found in wagons, which is similar to a "bone crusher" chassis.

Gottlieb Daimler used a new engine that was invented by engineer Nicolaus Otto for his motorbike.

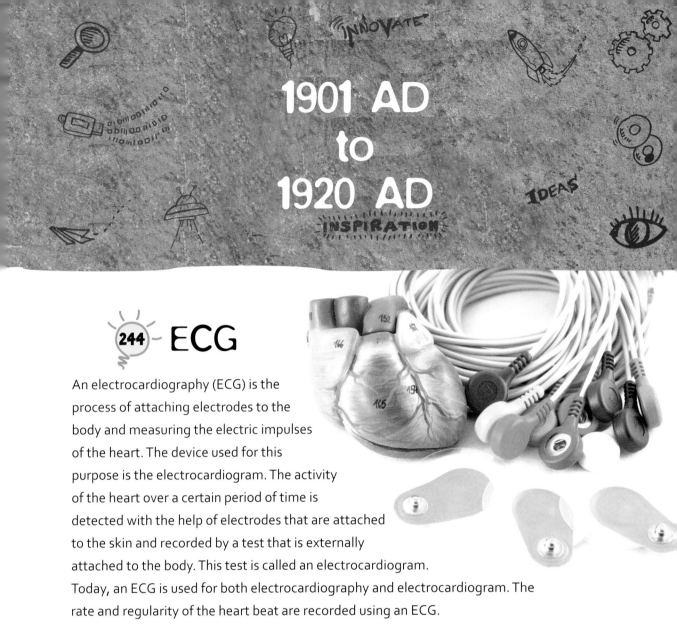

244 ECG

An electrocardiography (ECG) is the process of attaching electrodes to the body and measuring the electric impulses of the heart. The device used for this purpose is the electrocardiogram. The activity of the heart over a certain period of time is detected with the help of electrodes that are attached to the skin and recorded by a test that is externally attached to the body. This test is called an electrocardiogram. Today, an ECG is used for both electrocardiography and electrocardiogram. The rate and regularity of the heart beat are recorded using an ECG.

Willem Einthoven was the person to invent the ECG. He constantly struggled to design an electrocardiogram from 1889. In 1903, he successfully published the first electrocardiogram, which was recorded on a string galvanometer.

On 22 March, 1905, Einthoven began transmitting electrocardiograms from a hospital to his laboratory. It was during this year that the first electrocardiogram signalling was recorded from a healthy man. A significant number of his terminologies and original research remain crucial to electrocardiography even today.

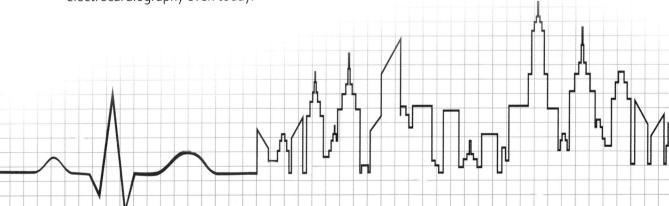

245 Popsicle

In 1905, the popsicle was invented by an 11-year-old boy named Frank Epperson. He initially named it the "Epsicle". On a cold winter's day, he had left his fruit-flavoured soda outside on the porch with a stir stick in it. He left it overnight and returned the next morning to see that the drink had frozen and stuck to the stick. He tried it and realised that it tasted good. It took 18 more years for Epperson to patent "frozen ice on a stick" in 1923, which was called the "Epsicle ice pop". His children later renamed it the "popsicle".

In 1925, Frank Epperson sold his famous popsicle to the Joe Lowe Company in New York. The rights to the popsicle are currently owned by Good Humour.

246 Photocopier

In 1937, a process called "photocopying" was invented by an American named Chester Carlson. He was originally a patent attorney, but also conducted part-time research and worked on his inventions. He invented a copying process that was based on electrostatic energy.

Carlson conducted photocopying experiments in his kitchen. He created his first photocopy using a zinc plate that was coated with sulphur. He wrote "10-22-38 Astoria" on a microscope slide and placed it on some more sulphur under a bright light. When he removed the slide, he noticed that it had left a mirror image of the words behind.

Carlson improvised on his invention and sold it to Joseph C. Wilson, owner of the Xerox Corporation, in 1946. Wilson is often credited to be the founder of "xerox". The Xerox photocopier grew so popular that "xerox" became a household name for the machine.

 247 Tar

Tarmac, or tar macadam, is a kind of road surfacing material that was patented by Edgar Purnell Hooley in 1901. However, the person behind the invention of tarmac was Scotsman John McAdam. He invented the method of crushed-stone road surfaces, but he was not successful in making the stones stick to the road. This was fine during the days when horse-drawn vehicles were used, but when cars arrived, the surface needed improvement. The rough material often led to punctures. During monsoon, many roads turned impassable due to ruts and mud. In 1901, McAdam was walking in Denby, Derbyshire, when he noticed a smooth stretch of road. He asked the locals why the road was so smooth. He was told that a barrel of tar fell from a dray and burst open. Someone had poured waste slag from the nearby furnaces to cover up the mess. By 1902, Hooley patented the process of heating tar, adding slag to the mix and breaking stones within the mixture to form a smooth road surface.

 248 Air Conditioning

The first systems that used water to cool indoor spaces were created by the ancient Egyptians. They would hang wet mats over their doorways to cool the air inside their homes. In 1820, British inventor Michael Faraday was experimenting with the refrigeration properties of gases when he discovered that by compressing and liquidising ammonia, and allowing it to evaporate, the air inside his laboratory cooled. In 1902, a young engineer named Willis Carrier created a system that was first installed in 1922 at Grauman's Metropolitan Theatre in Los Angeles. The conditioned air was supplied from the ceiling and exhausted at floor level. By 1903, Carrier designed a system of chilled coils that maintained a constant and comfortable humidity of 55% inside the Sackett-Wilhelms printing plant. This was the birth of the modern air conditioner.

249 Brassiere

The first modern brassiere to receive a patent was invented in 1913 by a New York socialite named Mary Phelps Jacob. She had just purchased a sheer evening gown for one of her social events. At that time, the only undergarment that was worn was a corset, which was stiffened with whaleback bones. Mary found that the whalebones poked out visibly from the plunging neckline and under the sheer fabric. She used two silk handkerchiefs and a pink ribbon to design an alternative to the corset, thereby giving birth to the brassiere.

250 Laparoscopy

Hans Christian Jacobaeus is credited with performing the first clinical laparoscopic surgery in Stockholm. This method was based on the experiments of Georg Kelling, a German physician from Dresden, who performed the first laparoscopic intervention in 1901 using a Nitz cystoscope on a dog. Jacobaeus published his initial experiences with laparoscopic surgery in the Münchner Medizinischen Wochenschrift under the title, "The Possibilities for Performing Cystoscopy in Examinations of Serous Cavities" in 1910. This procedure was used to investigate cases of abdominal pain.

251 Aeroplane

Brothers Wilbur and Orville Wright were American inventors who are considered to be the pioneers of aviation. In 1903, they achieved the first powered, sustained and controlled aeroplane flight. They surpassed their own milestone two years later when they built and flew the first entirely practical aeroplane.

The Wright brothers built upon their invention by following the research of German aviator Otto Lilienthal. When Lilienthal died in a glider crash, the brothers decided to conduct their own experiments with flight. They set to work by trying to understand how they could design wings in order to enable flight.

Wilbur and Orville were studying birds when they observed that birds angled their wings for balance and control. They tried to copy this principle by developing a concept called "wing warping". When they added a moveable rudder to the wings of their invention, they were successful in flying the first controlled power-driven flight. Wilbur flew their plane for 59 seconds at a height of 852 feet, which was an extraordinary achievement.

252 Band-Aid

In 1920, the first band-aid was invented by Thomas Anderson and Earle Dickson, an employee of Johnson & Johnson. Dickson invented the band-aid for his wife Josephine Dickson, who would accidentally cut and burn herself on a regular basis while cooking. This product enabled his wife to dress her wounds without any help.

Dickson, a Highland Park, New Jersey resident at the time, shared the idea with his employer, who was impressed by the idea. He began to manufacture and market the product as "Band-Aid". The first bandages to be produced were handmade and not very popular. By 1924, Johnson & Johnson introduced the first machine that produced sterilised Band-Aids.

In 1951, the first decorative Band-Aids were introduced to the market.

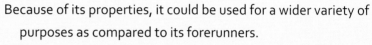

253 Bakelite

In 1909, a Belgian chemist named Leo Baekeland was responsible for creating the first completely synthetic plastic. This creation revolutionised the manner in which many consumer goods were produced. Baekeland called his plastic "Bakelite".

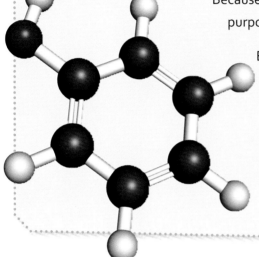

Because of its properties, it could be used for a wider variety of purposes as compared to its forerunners.

Bakelite was resistant to heat and did not conduct electricity. Therefore, it was a good insulator, which made it specifically useful in the automotive and electrical industries that emerged during the early 1900s. Bakelite was light in weight and durable. Additionally, it could be moulded into infinite shapes. As a result, its use quickly expanded as manufacturers realised its potential.

254 Wooden Swimsuits

Wooden swimsuits were invented in Washington in 1929. They were quite similar to the tyre-like swimming aids. However, it is not known who invented these swimsuits and how they came to be used. These barrel-like, wooden bathing suits were created to make swimming easier. The suits were made of thin spruce. They were considered to be practical as costumes and were also adequately buoyant to encourage a nervous swimmer to learn swimming. They were rather sturdy too, as they wouldn't warp or crack in the water. They were also adopted as a fashion statement.

255 Cartoons

The first cartoons to be screened were black and white. They had a tendency to be realistic drawings and models. However, people soon realised that this was the art of the impossible, where one could expand their horizons and create flying piglets, moving mountains or even dinosaurs destroying Earth! In 1902, a Frenchman named George Melies drew a "Trip to the moon", in which a spaceship hit the eye of the Moon Man, taking a step towards daring projects. Back then, making a cartoon took a considerable amount of time. A single animator had to make 24 slightly different drawings for each second of the animation, thus having to create 1,440 for every minute. By 1910, this technique changed and artists began working in teams, using "phase drawings" that were drawn on transparent sheets of celluloid.

In 1927, the first vocal movie was made in the USA and the sonic band matched the actors' movements. A young animator, Walt Disney, applied this for the first time to his cartoons in 1928. He created "Willie, the Steamer", a cartoon in which the famous Mickey Mouse made his debut. The character's whittled voice was that of Disney himself. He also created other famous characters such as Donald Duck, Pluto the Dog or Goofy. He was responsible for creating a strong connection between action and music.

256 Plastic Surgery

In 600 BC, an Indian surgeon reconstructed a nose using a piece of cheek. By 1000 AD, "rhinoplasty" was common, because of a custom that involved cutting off the noses and upper lips of one's enemies. During the 16th century, Gaspare Tagliacozzi, who is known as "the father of plastic surgery", reconstructed noses that were slashed off by swords during duels. He used

fragments of skin from the upper arm. This procedure was also used to correct the saddle-nose deformity caused by syphilis. The term plastic surgery, originating from the Greek word "plastikos", was coined by Pierre Desault in 1798 as a label for procedures to repair facial deformities. In the 19th century, the development of anaesthesia and antisepsis made plastic surgery safer and allowed for improvements in the technique. The first modern cosmetic rhinoplasty was performed in 1923, followed by the first public face lift in 1931.

257 Teabag

Thomas Sullivan, a New York tea importer, sent loose tea leaves to his clients in small silk bags in order to cut costs. Because of this, his buyers were more interested in having their brew pre-packaged in silk sacks instead of the loose form that they got otherwise. Sullivan did not realise this until many of his important clients began complaining about their orders not being in bags. As silk was expensive, he opted to used gauze sacks to package his blends and fulfil his orders. Thus, teabags were invented in 1908.

Leftovers from tea processing in the form of "fannings" and "dust" were used to fill the bags. Tea fannings were small, broken pieces of the leaf that could not be sold loosely, just as tea dust.

258 Zipper

The first appearance of a zipper can be traced back to Elias Howe, who founded the sewing machine. In 1851, he created a patent for a device called an "Automatic Continuous Clothing Closure". This device was similar to the modern zipper, although its structure was very different. The product functioned as individual clasps that were manually joined and pulled shut using a string that created a "gathered" effect. However, Howe did not continue developing his model.

After many years, another patent was created for the device. Forty years later, in 1893, inventor Whitcomb L. Judson devised the patent "Clasp Locker" or "Unlocker for Shoes".

259 Hair Dryer

In 1890, a Frenchman named Alexander Godefroy invented a hair dryer to be used in his salon. This was a sit-down dryer consisting of a large metal hood, similar to the ones that you see in hair salons today. Godefroy's invention included an escape valve for steam so that women's heads would not burn.

The machine and gas hair dryers that followed Godefroy's invention lacked the second element of modern blow dryers, i.e., airflow. However, in 1911, Armenian-American inventor Gabriel Kazanjian received the first patent for a hand-held hair dryer.

 Chainsaw

The first chainsaw was invented during the 1920s. The names that are associated with its invention are Wolf (USA), Westfelt (Sweden) and Stihl (Germany). The latter is the biggest and oldest chainsaw producer globally.

In the beginning, the intention was to make heavy forestry work lighter by using a machine. This would also lead to an increase in productivity, thereby resulting in profit. The first one-man chainsaw was produced in 1950 and was rather heavy. In 1959, the chainsaw weighed about 12 kg, whereas present-day chainsaws weigh around 4-5 kg and heavy duty chainsaws weigh between 7 and 9 kg.

 Hot Dog

One of the earliest references to the sausage appeared in Homer's Odyssey in 850 BC. As legend goes, the popular sausage, which is known as "dachshund" or "little-dog" sausage, was created in the late 1600s by Johann Georghehner, a German butcher. It is said that he later travelled to Frankfurt to promote his new product.

The invention of the Hot Dog is also attributed to the 1904 Louisiana Purchase Exposition. However, similar sausages were made and consumed in Europe, particularly in Germany, as early as 1864, and the earliest example of a hot dog bun dates to New York City during the 1860s.

262 Car Phone

Mobile phones placed inside automobiles gained popularity during the 1970s and through the 1990s, before a majority of the country had personal cell phones. The original car phone was invented nearly a century ago, when one man decided to travel across the country, tapping into phone lines from telephones that were set up along the road.

Car phones are not very popular today, but can be found in limousines and other commercial vehicles. In 1910, Lars Magnus Ericsson, an engineer from Stockholm, Sweden, installed a telephone in his car. As he drove around the country, Ericsson would use a pair of long electrical wires to connect his phone to the telephone poles installed along the road. While this was the first car phone, the concept did not gain any momentum.

263 Architectural Glass

Architectural glass refers to the glass that is used as a construction material in buildings. It is mostly used as a transparent glazing material in the building envelope, which includes windows in the external walls. Architectural glass is also used for internal partitions and as an architectural feature.

The glass used to construct buildings includes reinforced, toughened and laminated glass that is a lot safer than regular glass. Mies Friedrichstrasse is credited with creating the first glass structure in 1915. Prior to this, architectural glass had been in use for a very long time. Cast glass windows were a significant feature in many important Roman buildings as well as some villas in Pompeii and Herculaneum. However, they had very poor optical quality.

264 T-shirt

For a short period after World War I ended in 1920, author F. Scott Fitzgerald was the first person to use the word "T-shirt" in print. He included it in his novel, "This Side of Paradise", as one of the things that the main character takes with him to his university. In fact, minor tweaks to the design of early T-shirts were brought about at universities, which led to the invention of the "crew-neck T-shirt". These were created in 1932 by Jockey International Inc. at the request of University of South California. The university wanted a lightweight, absorbent garment for its football players to wear below their jerseys. This would avoid their shoulder pads from rubbing and chafing the skin. As a result, the T-shirt was extremely successful with the team. Soon, it gained popularity among other students too.

The T-shirt gained further popularity as an outer garment because of Marlon Brando and his role as Stanley Kowalski in "A Street Car Named Desire". Brando was seen wearing a tight-fitting, bicep-hugging T-shirt. His brilliant performance in both the play and the 1951 movie caused a nationwide increase in T-shirts sales.

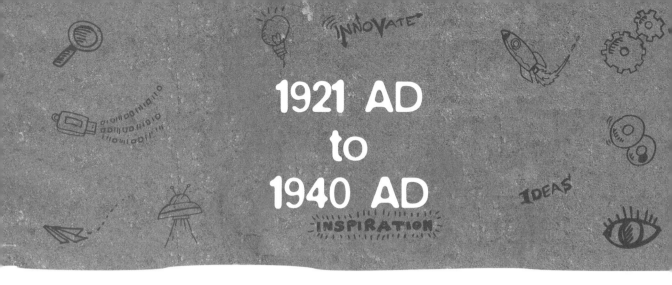

(265) Aerosol

The aerosol spray can was first invented in 1929 by a Norwegian engineer, Erik Rotheim, who designed an early aerosol propellant system. The can contains a liquid mix of particles that are contained under pressure in the can and let out as a spray. It was during World War II that containers filled with insecticide and propellants were used to safeguard US servicemen from insects that carried disease. Erik Rotheim was the initial forerunner of the present aerosol industry.

An aerosol system consists of four elements; active ingredients such as soap or disinfectant, inert ingredients such as water, propellant that pushes the mixture out of the container in the form of spray or foam, and a container that is usually made of steel or aluminium. The combined components work on the scientific principle of pressure difference mechanism.

266 Sticky Tape

Sticky tape also known as "masking tape" or "pressure-sensitive tape" was invented by Richard Drew in 1935. It is a type of pressure-sensitive adhesive, which is made from easy-to-tear, thin paper. The adhesive property enables the tape to get peeled off easily without leaving residue or damaging the surface on which it is applied.

Drew invented the sticky tape initially as a requirement for painters. Prior to its invention, painters used butcher paper. But the strong adhesive on it would peel off the paint during its removal, which would damage the painting. Drew felt that a gentler adhesive tape was needed and sticky tape was invented. During the 20th century, people began using the tape commercially.

267 Blender

In 1922, Polish-American Stephen Poplawski, owner of the Stevens Electric Company, invented the blender. It is a small electric appliance that consists of a tall container and blades. These blades perform the tasks of chopping, grinding, blending and puréeing food and beverages.

Stephen Poplawski was the first to put a spinning blade at the bottom of a container. He used his appliance to make soda fountain drinks. In 1935, Fred Osius improved on Poplawski's creation and invented the famous Waring Blender.

In 1910, L.H. Hamilton, Chester Beach and Fred Osius formed the Hamilton Beach Manufacturing Company that became popular for its kitchen appliances. Later, Fred Osius began working on ways to upgrade the Poplawski blender.

268 Insulin

In 1920, Canadian scientist Dr Frederick Banting wanted to create a pancreatic extract, which he hoped would consist of anti-diabetic qualities. In 1921, at the University of Toronto, Canada, in association with a medical student named Charles Best, he managed to create the pancreatic extract. Their method involved tying a string around the pancreatic duct.

When this extract was examined after several weeks, the digestive pancreatic cells had died and been absorbed by the immune system. Thousands of islets were left behind as a result of this process. Banting and Best isolated the extracts from the islets and produced "isletin". This creation later came to be known as "insulin".

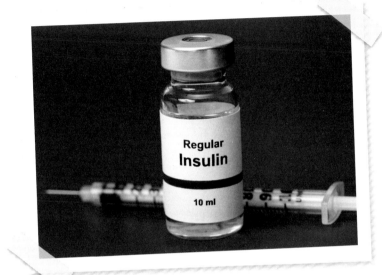

269 Lipstick

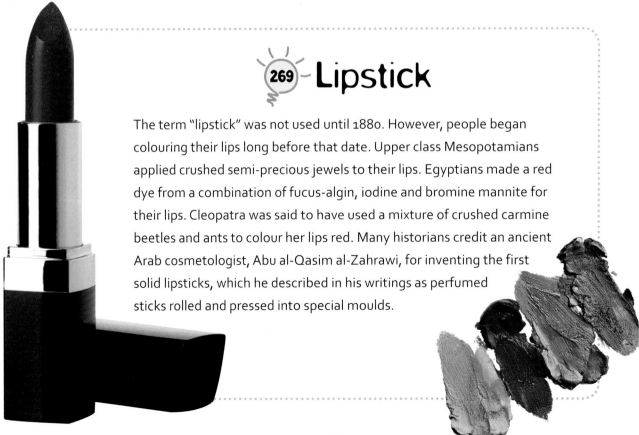

The term "lipstick" was not used until 1880. However, people began colouring their lips long before that date. Upper class Mesopotamians applied crushed semi-precious jewels to their lips. Egyptians made a red dye from a combination of fucus-algin, iodine and bromine mannite for their lips. Cleopatra was said to have used a mixture of crushed carmine beetles and ants to colour her lips red. Many historians credit an ancient Arab cosmetologist, Abu al-Qasim al-Zahrawi, for inventing the first solid lipsticks, which he described in his writings as perfumed sticks rolled and pressed into special moulds.

 # Chocolate Chip Cookies

Chocolate chip cookies were invented by Ruth Graves Wakefield in the 1930s. Ruth and her husband, Kenneth, ran the Toll House Inn on Route 18 near Whitman, Massachusetts, USA. Mrs Wakefield, a dietician and food lecturer, prepared food for the guests and was locally renowned for her impressive desserts. One day, while making cookies, she was out of an ingredient and substituted it with a semisweet chocolate bar. However, the chopped-up bar did not melt and mix into the batter. The small pieces of chocolate only softened and the chocolate chip cookie was born. These original cookies proved to be such a scrumptious success that Ruth repeated the recipe. She called it the "Chocolate Crunch Cookie" and published it in several newspapers.

 # Radar

Radar first appeared in 1904, invented by Christian Huelsmeyer, an engineer from Germany. The device that he created could detect an object that was 3,000 m away. However, it wasn't until Sir Robert Alexander Watson-Watt showed the maximum potential of the radar to the British Ministry in 1935 that it became the first detection system to be used in battle.

During World War II, this technology was being developed rapidly. There was a race between Britain and Germany to see who could produce the best radar systems for their national defences. The British won and completely utilised the power of radar technology.

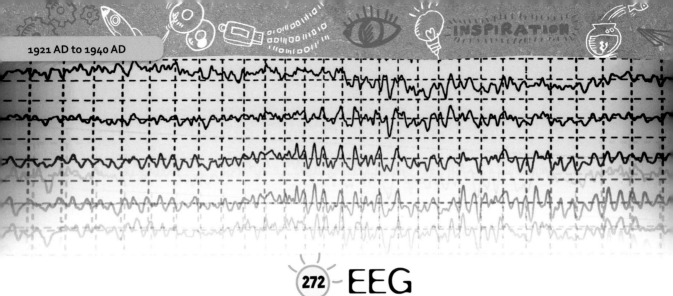

272 - EEG

An electroencephalogram (EEG) is a graphic picture of the electrical activity of the brain. Hans Berger was a German psychiatrist who developed the first human EEG in 1929. Berger was interested in psychophysiology. He decided to measure the brain's electrical activity so that the physiological record would provide an insight into mental processes.

Berger began his research for the human EEG by experimenting with dogs. He moved on to humans and began placing needle electrodes beneath the scalp of patients who had lost some of their skull bones in surgery. It was while working with one of these patients that Berger recorded the first human EEG.

273 The Isolator

Somewhere between 1913 and 1929, one of the pioneers of science fiction, Hugo Gernsback, invented a unique helmet to increase the concentration of his workers. The helmet, called "the isolator", was designed to improve an employee's focus at work by eliminating any kind of external noise. This uniquely devised helmet had only two components; a very small horizontal slit for a limited vision range and a pipe coming out of the helmet, which was attached to an oxygen tank. This enabled the person to breathe. This invention was introduced to the world by Hugo in the July 1925 issue of the "Science and Invention" magazine.

274 Missile

The word missile comes from the Latin verb "mittere", which means "to send". The first missiles to be used were a series developed by Nazi Germany during World War II. The most famous missiles are the V-1 flying bomb and the V-2.

Missiles target in several ways, the most common way involves some form of radiation, such as infrared, lasers or radio waves, to guide the missile onto its target. This radiation may originate from the target . It may be provided by the missile itself or by a third party.

Missiles are intended for damaging other ships and structures. They can hit moving targets and are classified as "guided" or "unguided". Missiles are of various sizes. There are two types of missiles: a short-ranged, high-damage weapon and a longer-ranged, low-damage weapon. The former is referred to as unguided and the latter as guided.

275 Hamblin Glasses

"Hamblin glasses" were invented in 1936 by Charles Leonard Hamblin. The purpose of these glasses was to make it easier for people to read while they lay in bed. Prisms mounted in the frames of these eyeglasses bend the light rays at right angles. These glasses had prism mirrors that were pointed downwards at an angle to provide a view that was lower than the usual line of sight. This enabled the wearer to lie down flat and read a book held upright on his/her chest.

The glasses were also ideal for rock climbers and anyone else who needed to see high horizons comfortably without craning their neck at an awkward angle. For example, you could use it whenever you want to enjoy a movie on TV whilst lying in bed or if you are a window cleaner, car mechanic, painter, cyclist and so on. Anyone who used these glasses, could view things comfortably and safely.

276 Computer

A computer brings the world closer and performs lots of tasks. It has eased our lives greatly and we have a German genius named Konrad Zuse to thank for it. Zuse invented the "Z1" in his parents' living room between 1936 and 1938. His invention is considered to be the first electro-mechanical, binary, programmable computer, which is the first functional computer.

The "Turing" machine, that was first proposed by Alan Turing in 1936, laid the foundation for theories related to computing and computers. The machine was a device that printed symbols on a paper tape in a manner that resembled a person following a series of logical instructions. Without these fundamentals, we would not have the computers that we use today.

277 Yellow Fever Vaccine

After several attempts to create a bacteria-based vaccine, the discovery of a viral agent causing yellow fever and its isolation in monkeys opened a new field of research. In 1951, Max Theiler of the Rockefeller Foundation received the Nobel Prize in Physiology or Medicine for his discovery of an effective vaccine against yellow fever, whose discovery was reported 70 years before. This was the first and only Nobel Prize given for the development of a virus vaccine. Recently released Nobel archives reveal how the advances in the yellow fever vaccine field were evaluated more than 50 years ago and how this led to a Nobel Prize for Max Theiler.

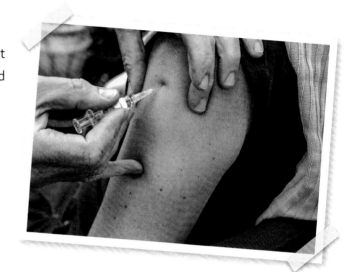

278 pH Meter

The pH of a substance demonstrates how many hydrogen ions it forms in a certain volume of water. The first pH meter was created in 1934 by Arnold Beckman. A glass pH electrode was constructed much earlier in 1906 by Fritz Haber and Zygmunt Klemensiewicz, but the technical difficulties prevented the large scale use of the "potentiometric measurements" of the pH. The main problem was caused by large internal resistance of glass electrodes, which made measurements very difficult. To obtain reliable results, one had to use a very sensitive galvanoscope, which was expensive and difficult to maintain. To overcome the problem, Arnold Beckman proposed to use a simple, high-gain amplifier consisting of two vacuum tubes.

279 Television

The invention of the television cannot be credited to one single person. It occurred across several stages. Two names have been considered as the pillars of this grand invention. The first credit goes to John Logie Baird who was the first to demonstrate a working television in the 1920s. He was an engineer by profession and was known as "The Father of Television".

The next is Charles Francis Jenkins, who invented a mechanical television system on 14th June, 1923. This system was the first of its kind and was called "radiovision". After this invention, he performed the first ever television broadcast transmission two years later in 1925 from Virginia to Washington. This was when the television first became commercially accessible in a simple form after a significant amount of experimentation. However, it was only after World War II that it began gaining popularity on a larger scale. Television as a telecommunication medium is majorly a platform for entertainment, news and

280 Sliced Bread

Sliced bread is a pre-cut loaf of bread that uses a machine for its convenience. Otto Frederick Rohwedder invented the first ever machine for bread-slicing.

In 1912, Rohwedder built a prototype of the sliced bread. Unfortunately, it was destroyed in a fire accident. Later, in 1928, he successfully came up with the final machine. This was known as the Chillicothe. The Baking Company of Missouri had used

advertisement. Since its invention, it has gone through considerable transformations in terms of technological advancements and specifications. The television has been one of the most revolutionary audio-visual inventions of all time.

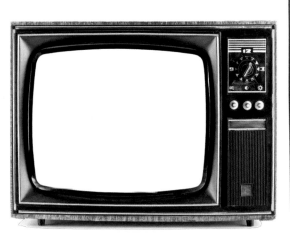

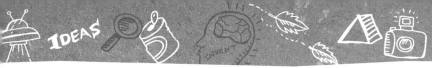

this machine commercially for the first time on 7th July, 1928, to make their very own first sliced bread.

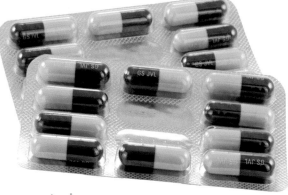

281 Penicillin

Penicillin was originally noticed by a French medical student, Ernest Duchesne, in 1896. However, it was rediscovered by bacteriologist Alexander Fleming while he was working in London in 1928. He observed that a plate culture of Staphylococcus had been contaminated by a blue-green mould that usually grows on bread. Colonies of bacteria next to the mould were being dissolved. On 14 February, 1929, Fleming introduced his mould by product called "penicillin" to cure bacterial infections.

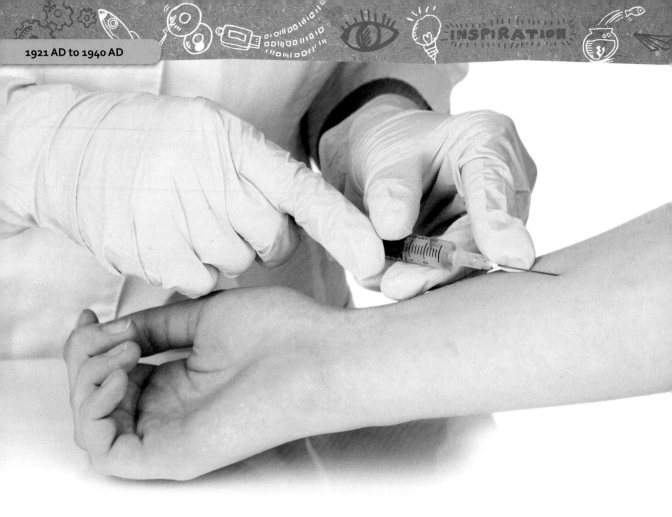

282 Tetanus Vaccine

Tetanus, also known as "lockjaw", is caused by a bacterium that is mostly present in soil, manure and the digestive tracts of animals and humans. Tetanus is not contagious and cannot be transmitted from one person to another. Bacteria enters the body through a puncture wound, which can be as small as a pin prick, or larger wounds made by rusty nails or dirty knives.

This bacterium does not survive in the presence of oxygen, which is why puncture wounds provided a perfect environment for tetanus bacteria to multiply and cause infections. They do not bleed a lot and are protected by tissue and skin from direct exposure to the air.

In 1884, Carle and Rattone first produced tetanus in animals by injecting them with pus from a dangerous human tetanus case. In 1889, Kitasato isolated the organism from a human victim and demonstrated how it produced diseases when injected into animals. Kitasato reported that the toxin could be neutralised by specific antibodies. In 1897, Nocard demonstrated the protective effect of passively transferred antitoxin. A method for destroying the tetanus toxin with formaldehyde was developed in the early 1920s by Ramon, which led to the development of the tetanus toxoid by Descombey in 1924. It was widely used first during World War II.

283 Atom Bomb

On 2 August, 1939, before the beginning of World War II, Albert Einstein wrote to the president of the USA at the time, Franklin D. Roosevelt. He mentioned that Nazi Germany was working on an attempt to purify uranium-235, which could be used to build an atomic bomb.

Shortly after this letter, the US Government began "The Manhattan Project". This project was committed to rapidly research on materials that would produce a viable atomic bomb. The chief person to unleash the power of the atomic bomb was Robert Oppenheimer, who oversaw the project from its start to the end. Until today, only two atom bombs have been deployed during warfare, both by the USA. These bombs were dropped on the Japanese cities of Hiroshima and Nagasaki on 6th and 9th August, 1945, during World War II.

284 Snowstorm Masks

A Snowstorm mask is a plastic cone shield that is designed to protect people's delicate faces from the severity of icy Quebec snowstorms. It was developed in 1939. It is considered to be one of history's strangest inventions. It is not clear how people breathe through these masks as they are completely closed. In Dutch, they are referred to as "Plastic sneeuwstormbeschermer". The inventor of these masks is unknown. Not much evidence is present on whether these masks were used for any specific period.

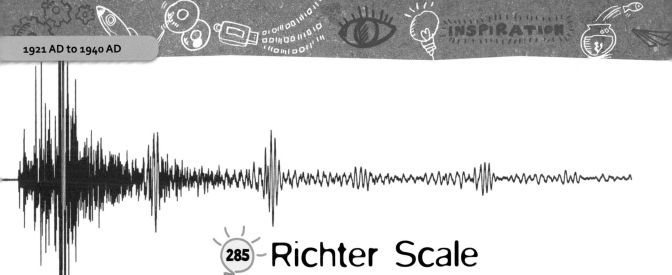

285 - Richter Scale

The Richter scale was invented in 1935 by an American seismologist named Charles Richter to quantify the magnitude or strength of an earthquake. Richter wanted a simple way to specifically express what is qualitatively obvious; some earthquakes are small and some are large. He wanted to quantify their impact with the help of the Richter scale.

On the Richter scale, the magnitude of an earthquake is expressed in whole numbers and decimal fractions. For example, a magnitude 5.3 may be computed as a moderate earthquake and a strong earthquake might have a magnitude of 6.3.

286 - Chemotherapy

Chemotherapy was first developed at the beginning of the 20th century. During World War II, it was discovered that people who were exposed to nitrogen mustard developed significantly reduced white blood cell counts. This finding led researchers to investigate whether mustard agents could be used to halt the growth of rapidly dividing cancer cells.

During the 1940s, two prominent Yale pharmacologists, Alfred Gilman and Louis Goodman examined the therapeutic effects of mustard agents in treating lymphoma. They conducted their experiments on lymphomas in mice, which proved that the tumours could be treated using mustard agents.

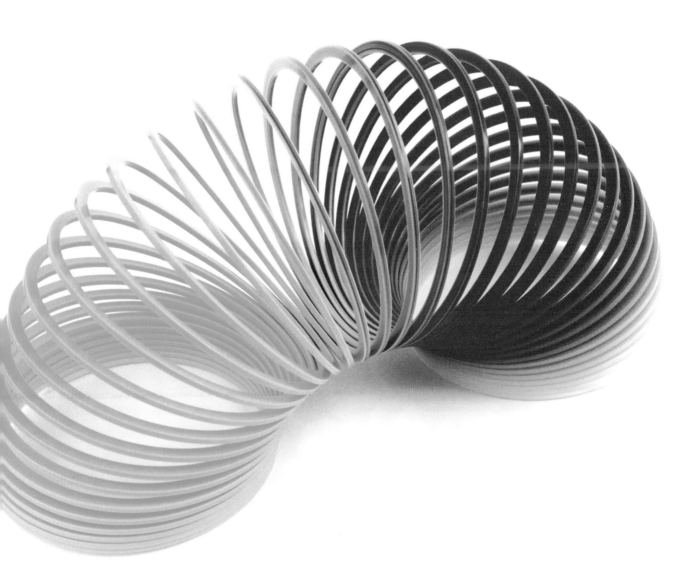 287 Slinky

In 1943, mechanical engineer Richard James was working to devise springs that could keep sensitive ship equipment steady when they were at sea. After accidentally knocking some samples off a shelf, he watched in amazement as they gracefully "walked" down instead of falling. This gave birth to the extremely popular "slinky".

Along with his wife Betty, James developed a plan to turn his invention into the next big novelty toy. Betty came up with the word "slinky". James designed a machine to coil 80-feet of wire into a two-inch spiral. The couple borrowed $500 to manufacture the first Slinky.

288 Teflon

You may have seen the "teflon" sticker on non-stick pans. Teflon is a brand name for "Polytetrafluoroethylene" or PTFE, a synthetic that is used as a coating on various pots and pans to prevent food from sticking to the utensil.

PTFE was discovered on 6th April, 1938, by an American chemist Roy Plunkett at the DuPont research laboratories, in New Jersey, USA. His discovery was accidental; Plunkett was working with gases that were related to Freon® refrigerants. While checking a frozen, compressed sample of tetrafluoroethylene, he and his associates discovered that the sample had polymerised into a white, waxy solid to form PTFE.

PTFE was first marketed in 1945 under the DuPont Teflon® trademark. The molecular weight of Teflon can exceed 30,000,000, which makes it one of the largest molecules known to us. The surface is slippery and virtually nothing sticks to it or gets absorbed by it. Therefore, Teflon was used as a coating on non-stick cooking pans. Teflon is a colourless, odourless powder that contains a fluoroplastic. It is known for having many properties with a wide range of uses.

Since DuPont's registration of the trademark, Teflon® has grown to become a well known household name. It is recognised globally for its superior, non-stick properties. These properties are associated with its use as a coating on cookware and as a soil and stain repellent for fabrics and textile products.

In 1990, US President George Bush presented the National Medal of Technology to DuPont for the company's role in the development and commercialisation of artificially-made polymers over the last half century.

(289) Helicopter

In 1863, French writer Ponton D'Amecourt was the first to coin the term "helicopter" from the two words "helicon", which means spiral and "pter", which means wings. The very first piloted helicopter was invented by Paul Cornu in 1907. However, this design did not succeed. French inventor Etienne Oehmichen built and flew a helicopter for a distance of one km in 1924. Igor Sikorsky is considered to be the "father of helicopters". Though he did not invent the first helicopter, he is given the title because he invented a successful design of the helicopter. All further designs were based on his design.

Igor Sikorsky's helicopters had controls to fly safely forwards and backwards, up and down as well as sideways. In 1958, Igor Sikorsky's rotorcraft company created the world's first helicopter that consisted of a boat hull. It could land and takeoff from water, and it could also float.

In 1944, American inventor Stanley Hiller Jr. made the first helicopter whose rotor blades were very stiff and made of metal. This allowed helicopters to fly at speeds much faster than before. In 1949, Stanley Hiller piloted the first helicopter flight across USA, flying the "Hiller 360", his own invention. In 1946, Arthur Young of the Bell Aircraft company designed the "Bell Model 47" helicopter, the first helicopter to have a bubble canopy.

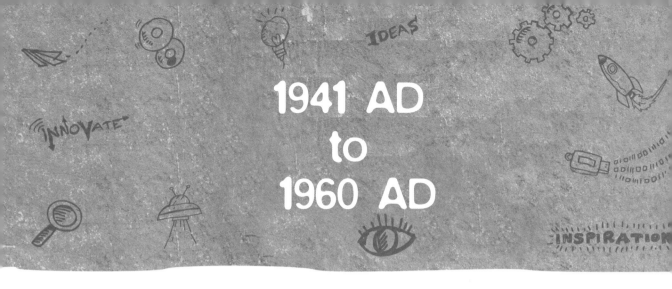

290 Velcro

In 1948, Swiss engineer and amateur mountaineer George de Mestral went hiking in the woods with his dog. After returning home, he noticed that the burrs clung to his clothes and his dog's fur. He wondered if such an idea could be used commercially. He studied a burr microscopically, only to discover that it was covered with tiny hooks, which allowed it to grab onto clothes and fur that brushed against it. After more than eight years of research and work, he created what we know today as "Velcro". It is a combination of the words "velvet" and "crochet". Velcro is made of two strips of fabric: one covered with thousands of tiny hooks and the other with thousands of tiny loops. The materials firmly stick together, but they also allow for an easy release.

While de Mestral's invention was ridiculed to a significant extent during its early inception, his perseverance enabled him to perfect the hook-and-loop technology for commercial use. He patented Velcro in 1955 and helped boost his company over other potential imitators. His company sold more than 60 million yards of Velcro per year during his lifetime.

291 Aqualung

If you have ever tried underwater swimming, you might be familiar with the Aqualung. It is the original name given to the first open-circuit underwater breathing apparatus. We now know it as a diving regulator. The type that was most familiar during the time of its conception was

the "twin-hose, open-circuit scuba". This was developed by Emile Gagnan and Jacques-Yves Cousteau in 1943.

Since its invention, several manufacturers have developed various designs of the aqualung and added many cylinders. The aqualung consists of a highly pressurised diving cylinder and regulator that supply the diver with breathing gas through a demand valve. This enables the diver to breathe comfortably underwater.

292 Magic 8 Ball

The Magic 8 Ball is a toy that is used for fortune telling or seeking advice. It is currently manufactured by Mattel. The device was invented in 1946 by Abe Bookman, who marketed and sold the device with Albert Carter of the Alabe Crafts Company. It was Carter who conceived the concept of a fortune telling device. However, it was Bookman who invented and designed the Magic 8 Ball.

In 1944, Carter filed a patent on the device and also added Bookman's name to the patent. Their revised creation was originally sold as "Syco-Seer: The Miracle Home Fortune Teller". The Magic 8 Ball contained a 20-sided polygon. This was placed inside a hollow plastic ball, floating in a liquid filled tube that was three inches in diameter.

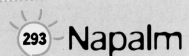

293 Napalm

Napalm is the thickener used for jellying fuel or other flammable liquids used in warfare. Napalm or "naphthenic palmitic acid" is an incendiary weapon that was invented in 1942. It is extremely flammable and is a fuel-based defoliant and antipersonnel weapon. It is capable of generating temperatures that exceed 2,000°F. The product was conceived during World War I when gasoline was used in flamethrowers. The problem with fuel was that it burned too quickly. During World War II, Harvard University researchers, led by Dr Louis Fieser, discovered that mixing rubber with fuel made it a longer-burning product; thereby inventing napalm.

294 Superglue

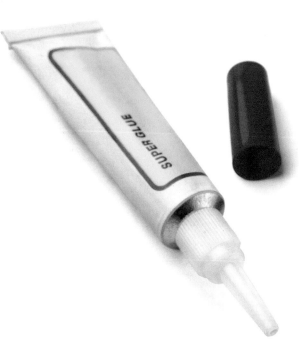

Superglue is also known as "cyanoacrylate". It was originally discovered in 1942 by Dr Harry Coover. Coover was attempting to make clear, plastic gun sights to be put on guns that were used by the Allied soldiers during World War II. One particular formulation that he created was not suitable for gun sights, but worked fantastically as an extremely quick bonding adhesive. Superglue was put on the market in 1958 by Eastman Kodak and was called "Eastman #910", though it was later renamed as "Superglue".

295 Microwave

During World War II, radar systems were installed to spot Nazi warplanes. One day, while working with radar technology, an American engineer named Percy Spencer accidentally invented the microwave oven, an appliance that heats food. While building magnetrons, he noticed that a candy bar inside his pocket was melting in front of an active radar set.

Spencer created the first ever microwave called "Radarange" by attaching an electromagnetic field generator to an enclosed metal box. The patent for this discovery was filed on 8th October, 1945, and the first commercially produced microwave was sold in 1946.

296 Transistor

In 1947, a team of scientists in Bell Telephone Labs, New Jersey, were working towards inventing a device that amplifies signals in electronics, replacing the existing vacuum technology. The result of several such experiments was the invention of a "transistor". The three pillars behind this invention were John Bardeen, Walter Brattain and William Shockley. They named their original patent the "Semiconductor amplifier: Three-electrode circuit elements utilising semi-conductive materials". The group was rewarded with the Noble Prize in Physics for their invention in 1956.

297 CCTV

The first closed-circuit television or "CCTV" system was developed in two parts. The first part consisted of the technology, which involved attaching cameras to live TV monitors. The second part dealt with the application, using technology for the purpose of security surveillance. In 1942, Walter Bruch, a German engineer, designed the first CCTV system. He wanted video cameras to monitor V-2 rocket launches. Siemens installed the system that he designed. At the time, there was no way to record the video feed. Someone had to watch the screen constantly to see what the cameras were noticing. This system worked fine for rocket launches.

Around 20 years later, someone thought about using this type of technology for security purposes. A woman named Marie Van Brittan Brown invented the first CCTV security system. She noticed that law enforcement officers did not respond immediately to calls. She wanted to ensure that homes were secured more effectively. She decided to use cameras and a TV to help solve the problem. CCTV security cameras were introduced in the USA by 1949 and were manufactured for commercial use.

298 Radio Hat

The early 1950s witnessed some cutting-edge technological inventions, one of which was the Radio Hat. It was invented by Victor Hoeflich. The radio hat was an inbuilt, portable radio set in a helmet that had the capacity of receiving stations within a range of an approximate 30-km radius. This was first commercially introduced as the "Man-from-Mars Radio Hat" in 1949 for $7.95. The radio hat was built five years prior to the invention of the transistor radio. Hence, the mechanism used in the radio hat was the existing vacuum tube technology.

The loop antenna and tuning knob, which were attached to the helmet, were visible on the outside. After the invention of the first prototype, the radio hat was gradually available in eight colours: tangerine, lipstick red, canary yellow, flamingo, rose pink, tan chartreuse and blush pink. Hoeflich's invention was the forerunner of the present headphones and portable radio. During the time that the radio hat was invented, battery-operated radios already existed, but Hoeflich's invention made it possible for users to wear it at any given time and place, and to listen to the radio in semi-privacy.

299 Supersonic Jet

The first aircraft to fly at supersonic speeds was a "Bell XS-1" rocket-powered research plane. It was piloted by Major Charles E. Yeager of the US Air Force on 14th October, 1947. After being dropped from the belly of a Boeing B-29 mother ship, the XS-1 broke the local sound level at 1,066 km per hour and attained a high speed of 1,126 km per hour. Thereafter, many military aircrafts of supersonic flight were built. The first supersonic passenger-carrying commercial airplane, "The Concorde", was jointly built by the aircraft manufacturers of Britain and France. It made its first Transatlantic crossing on 26th September, 1973, and entered regular service in 1976. The Concorde attained a maximum speed of 2,179 km per hour.

300 Lobotomy

In 1935, a revolutionary, legitimate medical treatment was invented for chronic mental illnesses such as depression and schizophrenia. A Portuguese neurosurgeon, António Egas Moniz ,coined the term "lobotomy" for the treatment. It was a form of psychosurgery. The surgery involved drilling holes in the human skull to access the brain, then cutting and scraping away the portions from the anterior part of the frontal lobes of the brain. Moniz received a Nobel Prize for Physiology or Medicine in 1949 for the "discovery of the therapeutic value of leucotomy in certain psychoses".

301 Polio Vaccine

American medical researcher Dr Jonas Salk announced the successful testing of a vaccine against a virus called poliomyelitis, which was responsible for polio, on 26th March, 1953. Polio is an infectious disease that causes a weakness in the muscles, usually in the legs. In 1952, the USA was attacked with this epidemic disease and around 58,000 cases were reported.

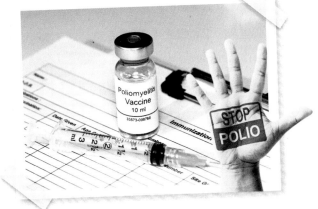

Dr Salk's invention of the first polio vaccine miraculously decreased the number of incidences to below 10,000 within two years of its invention. This vaccine was put to use by injecting a dose of dead polio virus in the patient. It was in 1957 that Albert Sabin invented the first oral vaccine for polio.

302 Kidney Transplant

Kidney transplant is the medical procedure of attaching a donor kidney inside a patient's body with an end-stage renal ailment.

The first kidney transplant between living patients occurred in 1952 at the Necker hospital in Paris. The procedure was performed by Jean Hamburger, although the kidney failed after three weeks of functioning. In 1954, the Boston transplantation was performed on 23rd December at Brigham Hospital by Doctors Joseph Murray, J. Hartwell Harrison, John P. Merrill and others. The procedure was carried out between identical twins Ronald and Richard Herrick to eliminate problems of an immune reaction. In 1990, for this and for his later work, Dr Murray received the Nobel Prize for Medicine. Sadly, the recipient of the kidney, Richard Herrick, died eight years after the transplantation.

INSPIRATION

303 Stairs

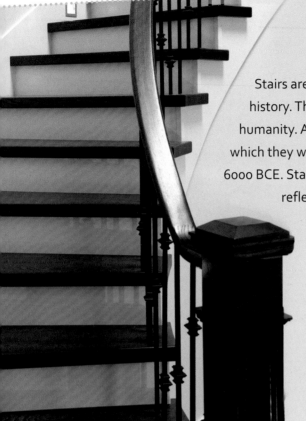

Stairs are one of the oldest constructions in architectural history. They have played a central role in the history of humanity. Although it is difficult to state the precise year in which they were invented, it is believed that they appeared in 6000 BCE. Stairs changed shape with changing architectural eras, reflecting the trends used in different ages and revealing the talent of those who designed them.

Stairs lead you from one floor of a building to another. They are a common fixture in contemporary architecture. However, they were invented only in 1948 by Werner Bösendörfer, a Swiss architect. The original invention was called the "stair steppes". Before stairs, people used ladders or ramps to move between different levels of a building.

304 Pacemaker

In 1950, Canadian electrical engineer John Hopps accidentally invented the early heart pacemaker, a device that could restart the heart by means of an electric current if it stopped working due to cooling. In 1941, while experimenting with radio frequency to restore body temperature, Hopps discovered the mechanism involved behind his invention. However, the device was too large to be implemented inside the human body; it was an external pacemaker. Wilson Greatbatch invented a new design for the medical pacemaker with a corrosion-free lithium battery to power it. This ushered in a new era in medical inventions.

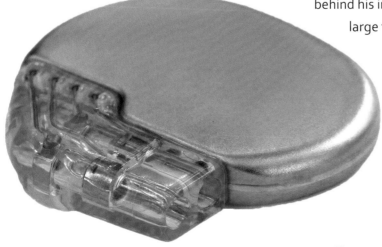

365 Inventions that changed the world

⚡305 Ultrasound

"Ultrasound" is defined as an imaging method that uses high frequency sound waves to capture precise images of different parts of the human body. Ultrasounds are used to detect tumours, analyse the bone structure or examine the health of a foetus.

Two names are significant in the history of the ultrasound. The first is an Austrian doctor, Karl Theodore Dussik, who published the first theorising paper on medical ultrasonics in 1942. The second is a Scottish professor, Ian Donald, who developed the first practical applied technology for ultrasound in the 1950s.

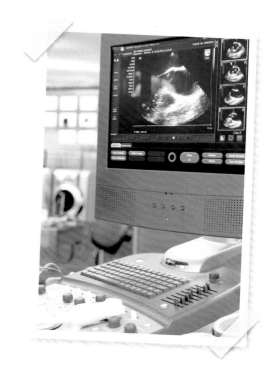

⚡306 Microchip

A "microchip" or an integrated circuit is defined as a set of interconnected electronic components such as transistors and resistors that are embedded on a tiny chip. This chip is made of semiconducting material.

The intent behind the invention of such a device was to increase the speed of electronic instruction flow by eliminating the distance between different circuits. Based on the early concepts of a microchip by German engineer Werner Jacobi in 1949, the first microchip was invented by Jack Kilby and Robert Noyce in 1957.

189

307 Barcodes

Barcodes were invented in 1948 when a food vendor sought help from Bernard Silver of the Drexel Institute of Technology to develop a method that automatically read product information and pricing. Bernard, along with his student Norman Joseph Woodland, began investigating and realised that the solution was a combination of ultraviolet sensitive ink and a scanner. Bernard and Woodland invented the first prototype barcode and filed a patent on 20th October, 1949.

The application was titled "Classifying Apparatus and Method". It described the invention as "the art of article classification through the medium of identifying patterns".

PRICE $11.50

12345 67890

308 Hovercraft

A hovercraft, also called an air-cushion vehicle, is capable of travelling over the surface of water by floating on a layer of air. The invention of this unique craft can be credited to Sir Christopher Cockerell, who created the design for the first commercially produced hovercraft called the "SRN1".

Cockerell tested the theory behind this invention in 1955 by placing an empty cat food tin inside a bigger coffee tin. He then used a hair dryer to blow air inside the tins. The result suggested that the hovercraft was able to reduce friction between water and the vehicle.

309 Dialysis

In medical terms, dialysis is the process of removing excess water or waste from blood. It is used as an artificial replacement for people whose kidneys have been impaired and are therefore unable to function entirely.

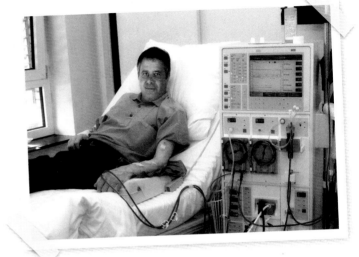

The invention of this revolutionary medical process is credited to Dutch physician Dr Willem Kolff, who invented the first artificial kidney in 1943. With barely enough material available, Kolff designed his initial crude form of dialysis to clear toxins from blood by using everyday items like orange juice cans, sausage skins, a washing machine and other common items.

310 Communication Satellite

A communication satellite is defined as an artificial satellite that is sent into space for the purpose of telecommunications. Its invention dates back to February 1945, when Sir Arthur Charles Clarke wrote a letter to the Wireless World magazine, predicting the future of his proposed concept of geostationary satellites. It was not considered to have potential at the time. However, his predictions came to be true on 12th August, 1960. The first communication satellite named "ECHO 1" was launched by NASA, marking an advancement in global communications. ECHO 1 was a gigantic balloon satellite with the ability to relay signals to other points on Earth.

311 Autorickshaw

The autorickshaw is a common mode of public transportation in many countries. It is also known as a three-wheeler, tempo, tuk-tuk, trishaw, autorick, bajaj, rick, tricycle, mototaxi, baby taxi or lapa. An autorickshaw is a three-wheeled cabin cycle for private use and is also used as a vehicle for hire. It is a motorised modification to the traditional pulled rickshaw or cycle rickshaw.

In 1947, the inventor of the Vespa, aircraft designer Corradino D'Ascanio, developed the idea of creating a light, three-wheeled, commercial vehicle to power Italy's post-war economic reconstruction. Autorickshaws in Southeast Asia began from the knockdown production of the Daihatsu Midget that was introduced in 1957.

In Japan, three-wheelers were not used after the 1960s. Autorickshaws are an essential form of urban transport in many developing countries and also serve as a novelty transport in many developed countries. In some parts of Europe, they remain a very important mode of transportation, especially in Italy.

Autorickshaws have a top-speed of around 50 km per hour and a cruising speed of around 35 km per hour, which is much slower than other automobiles. The triangular form of the vehicle makes manoeuvering rather easy, with the single front wheel dodging the available gap and the rear wheels enabling a larger space.

Video Conference

The process of video conferencing enables two or more people from different locations to communicate with each other face to face. Video conferencing includes both video and audio technologies so that people can simultaneously see and hear each other. The initial invention of video conferencing took place during the 1950s. Unfortunately, for the next six decades, the process underwent multiple innovations and advancements.

In 1956, AT&T came up with the first system that enabled two-way videoconferencing. The system was called the "PicturePhone". It enabled the communicating parties to converse with each other with a still picture being updated every two seconds. During the World's Fair in New York in 1964, AT&T presented a modified model of the system to the fair goers, but received a lot of criticism for their work.

It was only in 1970 that the further updated PicturePhone service became commercially available for the residents of Pittsburgh, Pennsylvania, USA. Even then, the system gradually fell apart because it was available at an extremely high service cost of $160 per month. This broadened the path for further advancements in structuring video conference models.

 313 Internet

The invention of the Internet was a group effort by several individuals. Its inception occurred in the technological advancement competition between the USA and the Soviet Union during the infamous Cold War. In response to the Soviet Union sending the first artificial satellite, Sputnik 1, into space on 4th October, 1957, the US government built the Advanced Research Project Agency (ARPA) in 1958. The creation of ARPA necessitated a dynamic way of exchanging data between different universities and laboratories.

Based on the ideas of Leonard Kleinrock's thesis of "Information Flow in Large Communication Nets" published on 31 May, 1961, this need was materialised by J. C. R. Licklider, who suggested creating an "Intergalactic Computer Network". This gave the theoretical basis for the invention of the Internet. His network enabled quick and efficient exchange of data between interconnected computer systems. The ARPANet was born and on 29th October, 1969, at 10:30 pm; the first Internet message was sent from KleinRock's laboratory at UCLA. This incident paved way for the invention of the Internet. The inventions that followed led to an advancement of the Internet.

Laser

LASER is an abbreviation for "Light Amplification by the Stimulated Emission of Radiation". Based on the theory of "Stimulated Emission" by Albert Einstein in 1917, Charles Townes and Arthur Schawlow invented the MASER (Microwave Amplification by Stimulated Emission of Radiation). The MASER was a precursor to the laser, but it did not involve visible light. In May

1960, following MASER, Theodore Maiman invented the first ever light laser called "Ruby Laser", which emitted short pulses of visible spectrum light. This invention revolutionised the fields of medicine, industry and entertainment with advancements such as fibre-optic communication, CDs, DVDs and many others.

Food Processor

A food processor is defined as a kitchen appliance equipped to process foods by kneading, grinding, shredding, slicing, mixing, blending and performing other functions. The first prototype was invented in 1960 by French catering salesman Pierre Verdon. He called his invention the "Robot-Coupe", which was renamed as the "Le Magi-Mix" by 1971. The original design of the food processor consisted of a bowl with a revolving blade at the base. The need for inventing this device came about when Pierre saw that different food processing functions consumed a significant amount of the clients' time.

316 BASIC
(Programming Language)

During the days of home computers in the 1950s, learning to work on it required a well-versed knowledge of the programming language. To fulfil that requirement, on 1st May, 1964, two Mathematics professors, John G. Kemeny and Thomas E. Kurtz of Dartmouth College in New Hampshire invented the first high-level computer programming language. They named it "BASIC", which was the abbreviation for "Beginner's All-purpose Symbolic Instruction Code".

The name makes the language very user-friendly. BASIC was successfully used for the first time to run programs on students' computers in Dartmouth College. Post its first successful run, the programming language was further implemented in different schools to run various programs. Both Kemeny and Kurtz believed that with the expansion of computer availability, the need for computer education would also increase. They wanted to ensure that students from streams other than Science and Mathematics would also pursue computer education. By the 1980s, BASIC was considered to be the primary language for home computers. It has also been the precursor for many other advanced computer languages such as Microsoft Basic, Visual Basic, QBasic and several others.

317 Computer Keyboard

The invention of computer keyboards is essentially linked with the world's first commercially successful QWERTY typewriter machine. The QWERTY typewriter was invented by Christopher Latham Scholes in 1873.

The initial alphabetic arrangements of keys on a typewriter machine created a lot of technical issues. In order to solve this, Scholes came up with the QWERTY design that served as the basic model for modern computer keyboards. However, in the 1960s, a couple named Bob and Joan Crozier realised the need for a pressing mechanism to use computerised technology. The Croziers produced the first ever keyboard keys.

318 Heart Transplant

A heart transplant is the procedure of surgically replacing an ill-functioning heart with a donor's heart on patients with end-stage heart diseases. An American surgeon, Norman Shumway, is considered to be the "father of heart transplant" after he successfully performed a surgery on a dog in 1958. However, the credit of the first successful human heart transplant goes to a South African surgeon named Christian Barnard. On 3rd December, 1967, he performed a heart transplant on 53-year-old Lewis Washkansky, who was suffering from chronic heart disease. The patient received a human heart from a 25-year-old woman named Denise Darvall, who died after a fatal car accident.

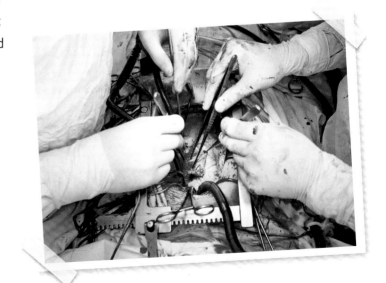

319 Glue Stick

A glue stick is a solid adhesive that is available in twist-up or push-up tubes. The mechanism of a glue stick, which is very similar to that of a lipstick applicator, makes it very convenient for the user to apply glue.

In 1969, a German company named Henkel invented the first glue stick under the brand name of "Pritt Stick". It offered an easy way to apply glue without getting one's fingers soiled or sticky. This cleaner way of using glue grew very popular with the invention of Pritt sticks. Within a span of two years, Pritt sticks were available in 38 countries, which increased to 121 countries by 2011.

320 Floppy Disk

A floppy disk, also known as a "diskette", is a flexible, removable magnetic disk used for data storage. The magnetic disc is encased within a rectangular plastic shell, which is lined with a fabric in order to remove dust particles. The first floppy disk was invented at IBM's experimental laboratory for data in California. Under the leadership of David L. Noble, a team of engineers worked on a project to develop a reliable yet inexpensive device for loading data for mainframe computers in 1967. As a result, the team came up with a magnetic material that was coated, yet flexible: a Mylar disk that could be inserted in the disk-drive slot.

In 1972, IBM received US patents for inventing the floppy disk.

Read about
Dr Spencer
Silver.

321 — Post-It Notes

Post-It notes or sticky notes are small pieces of papers that can be attached to other documents and different surfaces using the reusable strip of glue on the back. Their unique, low-tack adhesive allows the notes to be easily attached, peeled off and re-pasted without leaving any residue or damaging the surface that they are pasted on. The invention of Post-it notes can be credited to an accident. It occurred when a scientist named Dr Spencer Silver accidentally invented an extremely weak, pressure-sensitive adhesive called Acrylate Copolymer Microspheres in 1968, instead of creating a strong adhesive. This low quality adhesive was not of any practical use until 1974. That is when one of Silver's colleagues, scientist Arthur Fry, proposed the idea of using the low tack, pressure-sensitive adhesive to anchor his bookmark for his hymnbook. Arthur was a member of the choir and he would often lose the song page markers of the hymnal. Then came the Eureka moment; applying the adhesive on the back of the bookmarks solved Arthur's problem. This led to the invention of the final Post-It notes. The first Post-it note to be invented was yellow in colour as the laboratory only had yellow scrap papers to use.

Thank
Dr Silver for
inventing the
Post-It.

Find out what
led to the
invention of the
Post-It.

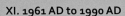

322 Pet Rock

The concept of a pet rock was invented by an advertising executive, Gary Dahl, in 1975. After gathering "pet" experiences from his friends, Gary conceived the idea of the perfect pet, a rock. Initially discarded as a "stupid idea", one of the key reasons for its eventual success was its packaging. The pet rock, placed on a straw nest, was packaged within a cardboard pet-carrier. It also came with a humorous manual on how to train and take care of the pet rock. The pet rock was launched for the first time at the San Francisco gift show in 1975.

323 Email

Electronic mail or email is a process of exchanging digital messages between an author and one or more recipients. Communication systems for computers were available in the 1970s, but they were very basic in nature.

In 1978, American scientist, V.A. Shiva Ayyadurai, invented a computer program at the impressive age of 14. It completely revolutionised the methods of inter-organisational and inter-office paper-based mail systems. He coined the term "email" for his invention. In 1982, Ayyadurai received the US copyright for email.

324 Bedazzler

A bedazzler is a device that is used to embed studs, rhinestones and patches on clothes and other materials. In the 1970s, it appeared for the first time as a direct follow-up marketing product and was invented by Herman Brickman. Brickman created this unique device in the shed of Ron Popeil, the owner of a company called Ronco.

The plastic device looks like a manual stapler. It has a base consisting of a circular wheel and plungers that are plastic-made applicators on the opposite side of the base. The rhinestones or studs are inserted into the device first. The fabric or any other material is adjusted to the correct position. The rhinestones or studs get imprinted on the fabric when the plunger is pressed against it. Sometimes, a bedazzler is associated with the retro or kitsch style of fashion because of the type of glittery clothes that can be designed using the device and also because of its low cost.

Ever since its invention, this one-of-a kind designing machine gained popularity among the users. The device made a special appearance on a reality show called "The Apprentice" hosted by Donald Trump.

325 Calculator

The hand-held pocket calculator was invented at Texas Instruments Incorporated (TI), in 1966 by a development team that included Jerry D. Merryman, James H. Van Tassel and Jack St. Clair Kilby. In 1974, a basic patent for miniature electronic calculators was issued to Texas Instruments Incorporated. The patent was for personal-sized, battery-operated calculators, with their main electronic circuitry in a single integrated semiconductor circuit array, such as the popular "one-chip" calculators. The first miniature calculator had an integrated semiconductor circuit array that contained all the necessary electronics for carrying out addition, subtraction, multiplication and division.

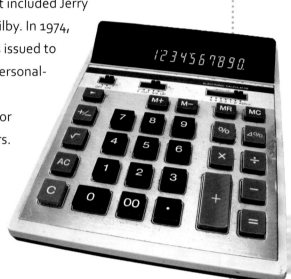

326 LCD

In May 1968, electrical engineer George Heilmeier and his team of scientists revealed Liquid Crystal Display (LCD) to the public. This is the technology that we see on computers, alarm clocks, cell phones, television screens, digital screens of microwaves and various other appliances today. In the scattering LCD, an electrical charge is applied to rearrange molecules so that they can scatter light.

The early displays were not up to standard, facing the problem of high power consumption, limited life and poor contrast. An improved LCD was invented in 1969 by James Fergason at Kent State University based on the "twisted nematic field" effect.

327 GPS

The Global Positioning System or GPS is a satellite network system, which orbits Earth at fixed points and sends back signals to Earth to assist navigation. A GPS system helps people get information about a particular place or time.

GPS was invented by the US Department of Defence (DOD) in the 1960s, during the Cold War. Originally, it was designed for military application. GPS was invented as a response to the Russian launch of spacecraft Sputnik for the first time in 1957. The US Department of Defence spent more than $12 billion taxpayers' money to create the GPS.

328 Digital Camera

In December 1975, Steve Sasson introduced the first digital camera to the world. Sasson was working at Eastman Kodak's applied research laboratory on a new device called charge-coupled device or CCD. It was a light sensitive integrated circuit, which was capable of storing and displaying data for an image. He created the first digital camera using a Fairchild CCD that transformed the received light coming from the lens into digitised numbers. To playback the stored image, data was read from it and displayed on a television screen. The first photo using the digital camera took 23 seconds to be created.

329 Cell Phone

Dr Martin Cooper, former General Manager at Motorola for the systems division, was the inventor of the first ever portable phone, a cell phone or a cellular phone in April 1973. He was also the first person to make a phone call from his newly invented, portable cell phone.

Long before its invention, the research arm of AT&T, Bell Laboratories, had introduced the core idea of the mechanism behind cellular communication in 1947.

The late 1960s and early 1970s marked a period when two leading professionals, Bell Laboratories and Motorola, became competitors to incorporate the two-decade-old concept into a practically applicable technology, i.e., a portable cellular device. The team, led by Dr Martin Cooper, designed the first cell phone and it was called the Motorola DynaTAC. The first prototype had a length of 9 inches and weighed about 2.5 pounds.

Cooper made the first phone call to Joel Engel, his professional rival at Bell Laboratories, to announce that he had invented the first cell phone. The DynaTAC 8000x was the first cell phone and was made commercially available in 1983. This invention revolutionised the telecommunication world.

330 MRI Scans

"Magnetic Resonance Imaging" (MRI) or scanning is based on a physics theory of the 1930s, called nuclear magnetic resonance or NMR. It is a method of examining the insides of one's body without any surgery or x-rays.

In 1970, a doctor and research scientist, Raymond Damadian, invented the basic concept for using magnetic resonance imaging as a medical diagnostic tool. Within two years of his invention, Damadian filed for a patent application titled "Apparatus and Method for Detecting Cancer in Tissue". In 1974, he received the first patent issued in the field of MRI.

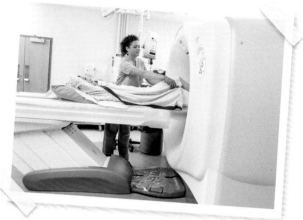

331 3D Printer

The year 1984 completely revolutionised the field of printing technology when the co-founder and head technology officer of 3D systems, Charles Hull, introduced the concept of solid imaging process known as "stereolithography" or 3D printing to the world. This revolutionary invention occurred when Charles was working on a project that used UV light to put thin layers of plastic coatings on furniture.

The first object that he created with 3D printing was a small, black, eye-wash cup. Based on the technique of stereolithography, the first commercial 3D printer was devised. It was also called SLA or stereolithographic apparatus.

332 Plastic Money

The first form of plastic money was a credit card, invented by a Brooklyn banker named John Biggins. It was introduced to the world in 1946. During its unveiling, John named his invention "Charge-It". Customers could use the card instead of cash to purchase items. Once they had purchased the items, the bill for the same was forwarded to Biggins' bank. Later, the bank obtained money from the customers after they had reimbursed the merchant for the purchase.

The conditions for using the credit card were: first, the customer had to have an account in Biggins' bank and second, the purchase was supposed to be made only on a local basis.

333 Space Shuttle

The invention of the space shuttle is rooted in World War II. During the 1930s, Nazi Germany started the "Amerika Bomber" project, an effort to build an aircraft that was capable of dropping a bomb on USA. An engineer named Eugen Sanger and a mathematician named Irene Bredt proposed the idea of a winged rocket called the "Silbervogel", but the project was never completed.

Based on their proposal, the National Advisory Committee for Aeronautics, NACA (the precursor to NASA) and the US military invented the first space shuttle. The space shuttle "Columbia" lifted off on 12 April, 1981, to mark the first space shuttle mission.

334 Genetically Modified Plants

During the 1980s, it was observed that specific pieces of DNA could be transferred from one organism to another. This was the basis of the genetic modification process. In 1983, the first transgenic plant, a tobacco plant resistant to antibiotics, was created. Later, genetically engineered cotton was successfully field tested in 1990. After five years, Monsanto, a leading company in biotechnology, launched herbicide-immune soybeans, also known as "Round-Up-Ready". Genetic modification was improved even further in 2000, when scientists discovered that the modification process could be used to introduce nutrients and vitamins to enrich foods. According to statistics, by 2004, genetically modified crops were grown by 8.25 million farmers in 17 countries.

335 Flash Storage

In 1984, Dr Fujio Masuoka invented the first kind of flash storage device while working for Toshiba. It was developed from EEPROM (Electrically Erasable Programmable Read-Only Memory). Two types of flash storages were invented; NAND and NOR, named after the NAND and NOR logic gates, respectively. Both the types were invented by Dr Masuoka. Initially called simultaneously erasable EEPROM, the term "flash" was given to them because of the storage's ability to erase a significant amount of memory in a flash. The NAND flash storage is used for general storage and transferring data in memory cards, USB flash drives and similar products.

336 Tamagotchi

The virtual pet "Tamagotchi" was invented by Naoharu Yamashina, a Japanese entrepreneur who founded the Bandai Company, a trendsetting toy manufacturer that produced action figures like Mighty Morphin Power Rangers during the 1990s. Tamagotchis are encased in an egg-shaped computer frame with an interface containing buttons. They are an alien species that deposited an egg on Earth to see what life was like. It is up to the player to raise the egg into an adult creature. The game was initially designed for girls to give them an idea of child care.

337 Digital Projector

The first digital projector was invented by Gene Dolgoff. He was working on a project in 1968 to come up with a video projector that would be brighter than the existing 3-Cathod Ray Tube (CRT) projectors. The idea was to use a filter such as a "light valve" to control the amount of light passing through the tube. Using such a valve would ensure the usage of a strong external light source. After conducting several experiments, Dolgoff narrowed down on liquid crystals for light modulation. In 1984, Goldoff introduced the first liquid crystal display or LCD projector to the world.

(338) Fibre Optics

The principle that makes fibre optics possible was first demonstrated by Daniel Colladon and Jacques Babinet during the 1840s in Paris. Dr Robert Maurer, Dr Peter Schultz and Dr Donald Keck invented the first optical fibre in 1970. Inspired by their belief that information could be transmitted through light, Drs Maurer, Schultz and Keck spent four years experimenting with different properties of glass until they successfully created the first "low-loss" optical fibre for telecommunications use.

The invention of the optical fibre revolutionised the telecommunications industry as it enabled low attenuation or reduction of signal strength. It also offered limitless bandwidth over the length of the fibre.

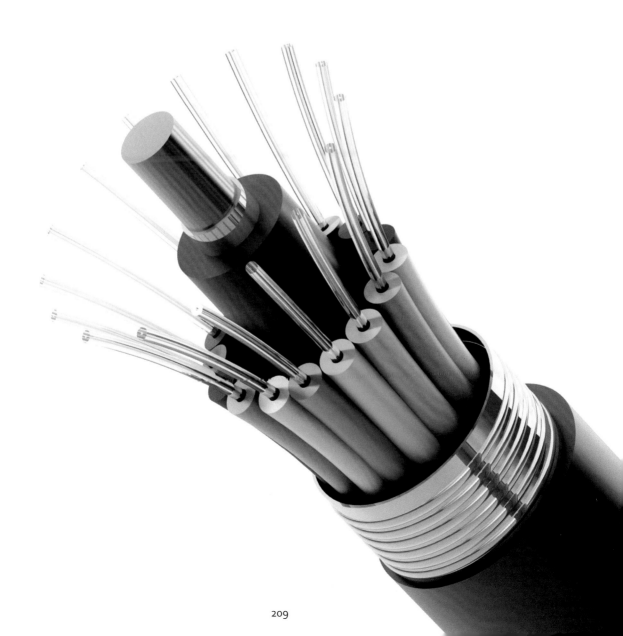

(339) Text Message

In 1984, the concept of text messaging was developed in the Franco-German GSM cooperation by Friedhelm Hillebrand and Bernard Ghillebaert. The first text message was sent in 1992 by Neil Papworth. Mobile phones did not have keyboards back then. Therefore, Papworth had to type the message on a PC. Papworth's text, "Merry Christmas", was successfully sent to Richard Jarvis at Vodafone. Later that year, it was marketed for person-to-person texting.

Earlier, GSM mobile phones did not support text messaging. The first message gateways for mobile phones were network notifications. Nokia was the first handset manufacturer whose GSM phone line in 1993 supported the user-sending of text messages. In 1997, it became the first company to manufacture a mobile phone with a complete keyboard.

Earlier, cell phone usage increased, but mobile operators did not focus on text messages and only focused on voice services, WAP browsers (Wireless Application Protocol for Web browsing on a mobile device) and handheld Internet applications. The carriers were shocked by the widespread use of text messages and tweaked their service plans to make the most of this revolution.

340 MP3 Player

Development of MP3 technology first began in Germany in 1987. A German Company, "Fraunhofer-Gesellschaft", began researching a program for coding music by using high quality and low bit rate sampling. In 1997, Tomislav Uzelac, an employee of Advanced Multimedia Products Company, created the first successful MP3 player after Fraunhofer's MP3 proved to be a disaster. Seven years later, Uzelac managed to produce a prototype as well as release the first MP3 player in the US markets. This was the first portable player of its kind and was known as the "AMP MP3 Playback Engine".

341 Cloning

The origins of cloning are not clear. However, the records of its use date back to the Middle Ages. Tissue culture was commercially used in the 1950s, mainly to reproduce orchids and it was used with other plants. This was a widespread practice in the 1970s.

The first animals to be cloned using embryonic cells were frogs. This occurred in the early 1950s. By the early 1980s, embryonic cell techniques were used to clone laboratory animals, which included mice and livestock such as cattle and sheep. By the late 1990s, researchers had developed cloning methods using adult animal cells.

In 1996, a lamb called Dolly was the first vertebrate to be cloned from an adult body cell.

342 Social Networking

Social media refers to Internet sites that provide a platform for people to interact freely. It allows people to share and discuss information about each other using a multimedia mix of personal words, pictures, videos and audio.

"CompuServe" was the first major commercial Internet service provider in the USA. It used dial-up technology and dominated the field through the 1980s. It remained a major player until the mid-1990s. CompuServe members could share files and access news and events. Additionally, it also offered true interaction. Today, social networking has reached an all new high, with several social networking sites now available for different purposes to people across the world.

343 Blogging

It is believed that the first blog was "Links.net" and was created by Justin Hall in 1994. At the time, it was not called a blog. It was only in 1997 that the term "Weblog" was coined by Jorn Barger, owner of the influential early blog "Robot Wisdom". The year 1998 saw the first appearance of a blog on a traditional news site, when Jonathan Dube blogged Hurricane Bonnie for The Charlotte Observer. In 1999, "Weblog" was shortened to "blog" by programmer Peter Merholz. After five years, Merriam-Webster declared the word "blog" as their word of the year.

344 Dog Goggles

The idea of dog goggles emerged in 1997 when Roni and Ken Di Lullo's Border Collie, Midnight, kept missing the Frisbee when they were playing fetch at the dog park. He was squinting a lot; Roni thought that it was because his eyes were sensitive to the sunlight. There was nothing available on the market, so she decided to customise a pair of sports goggles to fit Midnight. The shades provide eyewear protection and can help dogs with eye conditions that make them sensitive to sunlight. The idea worked and his Frisbee catching improved. Other dog owners at the park found it amusing when they saw him wearing goggles, but the idea soon gained popularity!

345 Edible Food Wrappers

David Edwards is responsible for introducing the concept of edible food-packaging. He created the "Wikipearl". The wrapping is held together by calcium ions and may

include particles of chocolate, nuts and seeds. The idea came about when Edwards, a professor of biomedical engineering at Harvard, had a conversation with a sculptor about the concept of "tensegrity". It is an interesting property and relevant for rethinking food packaging. Wikipearl ice cream and yoghurt were launched in selected Paris stores in June 2012.

346 Instant Messaging

"Instant messaging" gained popularity during the early 1990s, but the concept dates back to the mid-1960s. Multi-user operating systems such as the "Compatible Time-Sharing System" (CTSS), created at Massachusetts Institute of Technology's (MIT) Computation Centre in 1961, allowed up to 30 users to log in simultaneously and send messages to each other.

By 1965, the system had hundreds of registered users from MIT and other New England colleges. In the 1970s, programmers worked on peer-to-peer protocol, which allowed universities and research laboratories to begin simple communication between users of the same computer network.

347 Flash Drive

"USB" or Universal Serial Bus, also known as the "flash drive", is a protocol for connecting peripherals to a computer. The first USB technology was developed in 1995. It was co-invented by Ajay Bhatt of Intel and the USB-IF (USB Implementers Forum, Inc). The organisation comprises industry leaders such as Intel, Microsoft, Compaq, LSI, Apple and Hewlett-Packard. It supports and adopts comprehensive specifications for all aspects of USB technology. There are several flash drive producers all over the world. The storage capacity of flash drives continues to increase. The earliest versions of the USB could hold 8-128 Megabytes. Currently, 32 and 64 Gigabyte flash drives are common, and 128 Gigabyte flash drives are also available.

348 Moss Carpet

The moss carpet was invented by La Chanh Nguyen. It brings a little greenery into your bathroom in an unconventional manner. This living bathmat features three types of green mosses: forest moss, island moss and ball moss, which grow in plastazote, decay-free, recycled latex foam. As moss flourishes in damp, humid places, your bathroom is the ideal location for the moss carpet. This invention did not really take off as it does not provide any benefits. It has been invented in the last decade or so.

349 Diet Water

Sapporo Diet Water was launched in 2004 by a Japanese company. It had a successful launch and generated revenue above initial projections.

Out of 100 people who consumed the water for more than a week, an average of 2 individuals reported actual weight loss. Those who were losing weight have also been reported to have elevated levels of radiation in their blood. Unfortunately, these findings are inconclusive due to the small sample size. Learning to drink and like plain water is the best way to hydrate.

350 - Metal Detecting Sandals

As the name suggests, these sandals can detect metal while you walk, which allows you to find buried artefacts while walking on the beach. A copper coil is inserted into the right sandal, which is powered through a battery pack that straps onto your calf. These sandals use a copper coil in the right foot, connected by USB port to a base unit strapped to your leg. It can find metal objects in the sand up to a distance of two feet. It requires one 9-volt battery and works for up to six hours. These sandals were manufactured by Hammacher Schlemmer, a retailer and mail order dealer. The year in which these sandals were invented is not known.

351 - Hug Me Pillow

A dakimakura, also called the Dutch wife, is a type of large pillow from Japan. The word is often translated in English meaning "hug pillow". It is derived from "daki", which means "to embrace or cling" and "makura" meaning "pillow". In Japan, dakimakura are similar to Western orthopaedic body pillows and are commonly used by Japanese youth as "security objects". When and who invented these pillows is not known, but they are available online. They relieve pressure on the Lumbar and Coccyx (Hip), allowing the weight to be positioned at many levels of comfort while sleeping. Inserting the support system between the knees provides many levels of comfort for your hips and legs.

(352) Portable Chin Support

The inventor or date of the invention is unknown. However, the portable chin support has emerged since the last century. It is a portable device for supporting a human head while sleeping or resting in an upright position. It is a strip of flexible material on which the lower surface of the person's face rests. The strip works to provide a cushioned support and looks like a "hanging bridge". This is held upright by a stiff, vertical structure. One or more flexible straps provide stability to the structure. One strap, embracing the nape of the user's neck is considered necessary for any embodiment of the present invention. Other straps are connected to provide additional stability.

(353) Bow-Lingual

Bow-Lingual was developed by Takara Toys in 2002. It was created by experts who were working on acoustics and animal behaviour. Simply put, it translates your dog's messages for you in a language that you can understand.

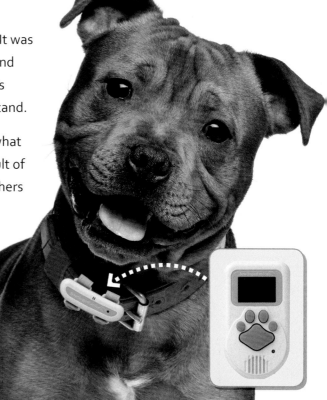

The Bow-Lingual uses voiceprints to determine what your dog is trying to tell you. Bow-Lingual is the result of many years of work by many organisations. Researchers created over 5,000 voiceprints of different dogs and determined that there are six fundamental patterns to their barks. They worked with animal behaviourists, veterinarians and dog owners to identify which emotion was being expressed.

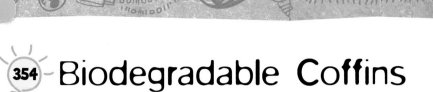

354 Biodegradable Coffins

Biodegradable coffins, also known as green caskets, are designed to satisfy the increasing number of individuals who prefer to have a "natural burial" rather than go through the process of a traditional funeral. Cremation was long thought to be an eco-friendly option, but many have been raising concerns about its excessive use of fossil fuels.

Biodegradable caskets can be made to bury someone in the ground or at sea. They do not harm the environment as they are eco-friendly and a cost-efficient burial option. These coffins do not use a vault or cement. Everything, including the hardware and lining, is completely made of natural materials. These coffins have been manufactured by an American company for the last decade.

Eco-friendly burials have been popular in Britain for many years, but industry experts say that it is starting to catch on in the USA, where "green" cemeteries are hosting natural burials. These cemeteries have increased in California, Florida, New York, South Carolina and Texas. Many people are opting for biodegradable coffins as they are environment friendly. There is no specific information as to who invented the first biodegradable coffin and when they did so.

(355) MySpace

MySpace is a social networking site that strongly focuses on music. It began in 2003 and was founded by Chris DeWolfe and Tom Anderson. MySpace grew in leaps and bounds. It became one of the largest online companies within no time. This happened because of a few people who were members of Friendster. They already had everything that they needed to get started and create MySpace. Some employees of MySpace were able to acquire equity in the company.

After a while, MySpace was bought by Rupert Murdoch's News Corp in July 2005. The company's name was changed to Intermix Media. It is now owned by American celebrity Justin Timberlake and Specific Media LLC.

(356) Air Conditioned Shoes

A Japanese company called Hydro-Tech created a pair of dress shoes for men that actually make them "cooler". But we aren't talking about personalities; we are talking about feeling cooler! These shoes were invented in 2011 and were called "The Cool Breeze". They are available in black or brown, but here's the biggest selling point – they are air-conditioned! These shoes were created for the company's Super Cool Biz campaign.

The company claims that the advanced filter technology keeps your feet refreshed and clean. These air-conditioned shoes are available online for a hot summer's day at about $78.

357 Android

Andy Rubin is the inventor of the Android operating system. He began working on the Android operating system back in 2003 when he started Android Inc., a technology start-up that tried to develop an open-source mobile OS based on industrial standards. Google acquired Android Inc. on 17th August, 2005. Key employees of Android Inc., including Andy Rubin, Miner and White, stayed at the company even after the acquisition. Today, Android is the most used mobile operating system in the world. Over 60 manufacturers use it; more than 750 million devices have been activated globally and over 25 billion apps have been downloaded from Google Play, a dedicated app store for Android.

358 Squirt Gun Umbrella

An umbrella with a water gun, more popularly known as the "squirt gun umbrella" is a concept that was designed by London-based designer Alex Woolley. This unusual umbrella was invented in 2011.

The umbrella has an opening on the top. The tip of the canopy is actually sunk in so it works like a funnel, passing the rain drops down into a squirt gun. The gun also acts as the handle of the umbrella. The water collected in the gun can be used to squirt all the people who do not have umbrellas!

The umbrella is more of a pranking device than a rainy cover. It may be a good idea to use this umbrella while going out with friends, but only if one doesn't mind getting into trouble for using it!

359 Snuggie

Snuggie is a wearable blanket with sleeves. It helps people keep the comfort of a blanket around them even as they move around. In winter 2008/2009, the Snuggie became a global sensation.

Snuggie was brought to the market by Scott Boilen, President and CEO of New York's Allstar Product Group, which sells the item. By 2013, more than 30 million Snuggies were sold, bringing in around $500 million for Allstar. Interestingly, the Snuggie was not the first sleeved blanket to hit the shelves. The "Slanket", invented by Gary Clegg in 1997, has been sold on QVC since 2007.

360 Instagram

Instagram is an online photo sharing platform where a person can edit a picture, add a particular filter from an existing set of filters and share it with multiple users. The platform also allows people to share their pictures across other popular social networking sites. It is for people to share pictures of anything they want. All they have to do is add "hashtags" to their caption and share it with the world. Instagram was created by two young men, Kevin Systrom and Mike Krieger, on 6th October, 2010. Kevin Systrom made $40 million in just 18 months, thanks to his creation.

INSPIRATION

361 Facebook

Facebook was invented by Harvard computer science student Mark Zuckerberg along with classmates Eduardo Saverin, Dustin Moskovitz and Chris Hughes. The website was originally and briefly called "The Facebook". Mark Zuckerberg was a second year student when he wrote the software for the Facemash website. In 2004, an angel investor, Sean Parker, founder of Napster, took over as the company's president. The company changed the name to just "Facebook" after purchasing the domain name "facebook.com" in 2005 for $200,000.

362 Twitter

Jack Dorsey was working on a solo idea and presented it to the company that had employed him as a web designer. This was called "Odeo". Odeo started as a podcasting company by Noah Glass. However, Apple Computers launched a podcasting platform called iTunes that was to dominate the market, making podcasting a poor choice as a venture for Odeo. In February 2006, Glass and Dorsey, along with developer Florian Weber, presented another project to the company. The project, initially called "Twttr" by Glass, was a system where you could send a text to one number and it would be broadcasted to all your desired contacts. The Twttr project got the green light and by July 2006, it was released to the public. The first tweet was sent out on 21 March, 2006, at 9:50 pm Pacific Standard Time, when Jack Dorsey tweeted "just setting up my Twttr".

363 Robot

The first version of a robot was actually invented around 400–350 BC! The inventor was a Greek mathematician named Archytas. He invented a steam-powered pigeon. The bird was made out of wood. Aided by steam, it was able to move around on its own. It was recorded to have gone as far as 200 m before the steam ran out. The first modern programmable robot was "Unimate". Unimate was an autonomous, pre-programmed robot that repeatedly performed the same task. In 1961, General Motors installed the first robot to work in a factory. It moved pieces of hot metal.

In 1966, "Shakey the Robot" was invented at Stanford. It was the first autonomous, intelligent robot that made its own decisions. Shakey could be given general instructions such as "move the block onto the table" and it would reason how to perform the task. This involved looking around the room, identifying the block and finding out how to move the block to the table. In 2004, Shakey was inducted into Carnegie Mellon's Robot Hall of Fame.

364 Mouse

During the 1960s, scientists who were researching advancements in computer technology required a device that would move around the screen and interact with the displayed information. There were devices such as a joystick or light pen, but they required something that was a lot more efficient. In 1964, Douglas Carl Engelbart invented the first prototype computer mouse. The first patented mouse was a wooden shell with two metal wheels. It had to be used with a graphical user interface. The patent described the mouse as the "X-Y position indicator for a display system". The term "mouse" was coined because of its structure.

365 Ostrich Pillow

The Ostrich Pillow is designed for the purpose of power naps. Its soft yet firm filling provides a comfortable cocoon anywhere. You can freely lean your head against metal poles, the back of a wooden bench or a granite countertop. Anything with a surface can be converted into a perfect napping surface with the Ostrich Pillow. It was invented by Kawamura Ganjavian Studios, the firm that Mr Ganjavian set up with a friend from university in 2000.

The Ostrich Pillow's interior is made from 100% viscose cloth, which is extremely soft, smooth and highly absorbent, but does not insulate body heat. This ensures that you remain cool and comfortable while you are asleep.

The filling for the Ostrich Pillow is popped polystyrene, which is similar to the filling found in bean bag chairs. This makes the pillow soft and pliable, but becomes firm when sufficient force is applied to it. It basically forms a protective envelope around your head while you nap. The Ostrich Pillow's filling allows it to conform to the shape of your head as well as what your head is resting against. Being sufficiently thick ensures that there is adequate cushioning so that you feel like you are sleeping on a cloud.

Index

1. 3D Printer 205
2. Abacus 58
3. Accelerometer 87
4. Aeroplane 156
5. Aerosol 164
6. Air Conditioned Shoes 219
7. Air Conditioning 154
8. Altimeter 132
9. Aluminium 111
10. Android 220
11. Antiseptics 115
12. Aqualung 181
13. Aqueduct 45
14. Archimedes' screw 41
15. Architectural Arch 37
16. Architectural Glass 162
17. Aspirin 149
18. Atom Bomb 175
19. Autorickshaw 192
20. Axe 14
21. Bakelite 157
22. Baking 35
23. Band-Aid 156
24. Barbed Wire 123
25. Barcodes 190
26. Barometer 82
27. Barrel 46
28. BASIC (Programming Language) 196
29. Bathtub 43
30. Battery 95
31. Bedazzler 201
32. Belt 18
33. Bicycle 102
34. Biodegradable Coffins 218
35. Blender 165
36. Blogging 212
37. Blood Transfusion 83
38. Bow and Arrow 5
39. Bow-lingual 217
40. Bowtie 79
41. Braille 105
42. Brassiere 155
43. Brick 5
44. Bronze 21
45. Bullet 75
46. Bunsen Burner 117
47. Bus 104
48. Butter Stick 125
49. Button 21
50. Cable Car 128
51. Calculator 202
52. Calliper 44
53. Camera 101
54. Candles 51
55. Cannon 61
56. Car 140
57. Car Phone 162
58. Carbonated Water 87
59. Cartoons 158

60. Catapult 46
61. Catheter 139
62. Cave Painting 6
63. CCTV 184
64. Ceiling Fan 121
65. Cell Phone 204
66. Cement 20
67. Chainsaw 161
68. Chariot 39
69. Chemotherapy 176
70. Chocolate Chip Cookies 167
71. Church 60
72. Cloning 211
73. Cork 79
74. Clothes Iron 76
75. Colour Photography 135
76. Columns 34
77. Communication Satellite 191
78. Compass 50
79. Computer 170
80. Computer Keyboard 197
81. Concrete 31
82. Cornflakes 147
83. Corset 72
84. Cotton Candy 148
85. Cotton Gin 93
86. Crescent Wrench 143
87. Dam 32
88. Dentistry 28
89. Dialysis 191
90. Diet Water 215
91. Digital Camera 203
92. Digital Projector 208
93. Dirigible 113
94. Dog Goggles 213
95. Dome 52
96. Dress 65
97. Dry Cell Battery 151
98. Dye 34
99. Dynamite 127
100. ECG 152
101. Edible Food Wrappers 213
102. EEG 168
103. Egg Beater 137
104. Electric Chair 142
105. Electric Heater 142
106. Electricity 69
107. Electrometer 130
108. Elevator 114
109. Email 200
110. Escalator 121
111. Facebook 222
112. Fax 114
113. Fermentation 12
114. Fibre Optics 209
115. Fire 2
116. Fishing Net 10
117. Flash Drive 214
118. Flash Storage 207

119. Floppy Disk 198
120. Flutes 7
121. Food Processor 195
122. Frying 35
123. Fur 4
124. General Anaesthesia 115
125. Genetically Modified Plants 207
126. Gloves 43
127. Glue 16
128. Glue Stick 198
129. GPS 203
130. Gramophone 139
131. Gregorian Calendar 76
132. Gun 63
133. Gunpowder 63
134. Gyroscope 117
135. Hair Dryer 160
136. Hamblin Glasses 170
137. Handbag 107
138. Hang Glider 97
139. Hanger 125
140. Harvester 107
141. Hats 75
142. Heart Transplant 197
143. Heeled Shoes 74
144. Helicopter 179
145. Hot Air Balloon 92
146. Hot Dog 161
147. Hovercraft 190
148. Hug Me Pillow 216
149. Hydrometer 59
150. Instagram 221
151. Instant Messaging 214
152. Insulin 166
153. Internet 194
154. Iron 25
155. Iron Bridge 91
156. Irrigation 14
157. Jeans 124
158. Jukebox 143
159. Julian Calendar 53
160. Kidney Transplant 187
161. Knife 3
162. Kohl 24
163. Lace 67
164. Language 11
165. Laparoscopy 155
166. Laser 195
167. LCD 202
168. Leather 15
169. Lever 52
170. Light Bulb 131
171. Light Meter 140
172. Lipstick 166
173. Lobotomy 186
174. Lock and Key 44
175. Log Raft 3
176. Macintosh Raincoat 104
177. Magic 8 Ball 181
178. Magnifying Glass 47
179. Matchstick 103

180. Mauve 130
181. Mayonnaise 86
182. Metal Detecting Sandals 216
183. Metal Detector 136
184. Microchip 189
185. Microphone 134
186. Microscope 73
187. Microwave 183
188. Milking Machine 135
189. Milling 53
190. Missile 169
191. Morse Code 108
192. Mortar 13
193. Moss Carpet 215
194. Motion Camera 146
195. Motorbike 151
196. Moving Pictures 127
197. MP3 Player 211
198. MRI Scans 205
199. MySpace 219
200. Mouse 223
201. Napalm 182
202. Ohmmeter 119
203. Oven 54
204. Ostrich Pillow 224
205. Pacemaker 188
206. Palanquin 51
207. Pants 29
208. Paper 57
209. Paper Clip 126
210. Paper Money 61
211. Papyrus 16
212. Parachute 84
213. Pasteurisation 133
214. Paved Roads 29
215. Pencil 70
216. Penicillin 173
217. Pens 23
218. Perfume 36
219. Pet Rock 200
220. pH Meter 171
221. Phonograph 134
222. Photocopier 153
223. Pigment 9
224. Pillow 12
225. Planned Language 129
226. Plastic Money 206
227. Plastic Surgery 159
228. Pliers 32
229. Plough 36
230. Ploughshare 27
231. Plumbing 50
232. Polio Vaccine 187
233. Popsicle 153
234. Portable Chin Support 217
235. Post-It Notes 199
236. Postal Service 55
237. Potato Chips 118
238. Pottery 10
239. Preservatives 9

240. Pretzel 62
241. Printing Press 71
242. Protractor 96
243. Pulley 48
244. Punching Cards 138
245. Quinine 97
246. Rabies Vaccine 137
247. Radar 167
248. Radio 144
249. Radio Hat 185
250. Railroad 78
251. Razor 86
252. Reaper 100
253. Refined Salt 13
254. Refined Sugar 40
255. Refrigerator 85
256. Remote Control 148
257. Richter Scale 176
258. Rifle 67
259. Robot 223
260. Rocket 64
261. Rope 8
262. Ruler 38
263. Safety Pin 113
264. Sandwich 89
265. Saw 20
266. Scarf 42
267. Scissors 39
268. Screwdriver 69
269. Sewage System 30
270. Sewing Machine 106
271. Sewing Needle 7
272. Ship 19
273. Shoes 17
274. Snuggie 221
275. Shower 42
276. Silk 22
277. Skyscraper 138
278. Sliced Bread 172
279. Slinky 177
280. Smallpox Vaccine 90
281. Snowstorm Masks 175
282. Soap 33
283. Social Networking 212
284. Socks 56
285. Solar Cells 98
286. Space Shuttle 206
287. Spear 4
288. Spectacles 68
289. Speedometer 149
290. Spinning Jenny 88
291. Spinning Wheel 66
292. Squirt Gun Umbrella 220
293. Stairs 188
294. Stamps 109
295. Stapler 111
296. Statue 8
297. Steam Boat 90
298. Steam Engine 80
299. Steel 40
300. Stethoscope 100
301. Sticky Tape 165

302. Stockings 74
303. Stone Tools 1
304. Submarine 80
305. Sundial 17
306. Superglue 182
307. Supersonic Jet 186
308. Suspenders 103
309. Suspension Bridge 110
310. Swimsuit 55
311. Synthetic Dyes 119
312. Syringe 116
313. T-shirt 163
314. Tamagotchi 208
315. Tank 150
316. Tar 154
317. Tattoos 24
318. Teabag 159
319. Teapot 72
320. Teflon 178
321. Telegraph 109
322. Telephone 131
323. Telescope 81
324. Television 172
325. Tetanus Vaccine 174
326. Text Message 210
327. The Isolator 168
328. Thermometer 77
329. Thresher 93
330. Tie 82
331. Tin Can 98
332. Toaster 144
333. Toilet 33
334. Toothbrush 58
335. Toothpaste 26
336. Torch/Flashlight 147
337. Tractor 99
338. Traffic Signal 122
339. Transistor 183
340. Tuxedo 120
341. Twitter 222
342. Typewriter 128
343. Ultrasound 189
344. Umbrella 38
345. Vaccination 94
346. Vacuum Cleaner 123
347. Vault (Architecture) 59
348. Velcro 180
349. Velvet 64
350. Vending Machine 132
351. Video Conference 193
352. Voltmeter 112
353. Watch 70
354. Water Frame 85
355. Waterwheel 49
356. Watt Metre 141
357. Weighing Scale 27
358. Wheel 18
359. Wheelbarrow 47
360. Wigs 23
361. Wooden Swimsuits 157
362. X-Ray 145
363. Yellow Fever Vaccine 171
364. Zeppelin 150
365. Zipper 160

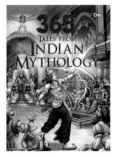
ISBN: 978-81-87107-46-0

ISBN: 978-93-52760-95-4

ISBN: 978-93-84225-31-5

ISBN: 978-93-80070-79-7

ISBN: 978-81-87107-53-8

ISBN: 978-93-83202-81-2

ISBN: 978-93-80069-36-4

ISBN: 978-81-87107-52-1

ISBN: 978-81-87107-57-6

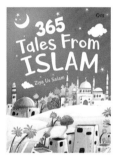
ISBN: 978-93-52764-05-1

ISBN: 978-81-87107-58-3

ISBN: 978-93-80070-84-1

ISBN: 978-93-80070-83-4

ISBN: 978-93-81607-57-2

ISBN: 978-93-81607-49-7

ISBN: 978-93-52764-06-8

ISBN: 978-81-87107-55-2

ISBN: 978-93-85031-29-8

ISBN: 978-93-52760-49-7

ISBN: 978-93-52760-96-1

ISBN: 978-93-84225-33-9

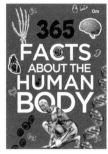
ISBN: 978-93-84625-93-1

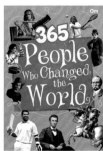
ISBN: 978-93-84225-34-6

ISBN: 978-81-87107-56-9

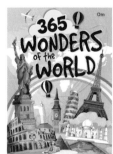
ISBN: 978-93-80069-35-7